10.99

The Art School

OIL PAINTING
PORTRAITS

0 57812 23910 4

The Art School

OIL PAINTING
PORTRAITS

RAY SMITH

PRENTICE HALL CANADA INC.,
SCARBOROUGH, ONTARIO

A DORLING KINDERSLEY BOOK

Editor Louise Candlish
Art editor Claire Pegrum
Designer Dawn Terrey
Assistant editor Margaret Chang
Series editor Emma Foa
Managing editor Sean Moore
Managing art editor Toni Kay
DTP designer Zirrinia Austin
Production controller Helen Creeke
Photography Steve Gorton,
Andy Crawford, Tim Ridley

First published in Canada in 1994 by
Prentice Hall Canada Inc.,
Scarborough, Ontario.

This DK Art School book first published in
Great Britain in 1994 by Dorling Kindersley Limited
9 Henrietta Street, London WC2E 8PS

Copyright © 1994

Dorling Kindersley Limited, London

Canadian Cataloguing in Publication Data

Smith, Ray, 1949–
Oil painting portraits

(The Art school)
Includes index.
ISBN 0-13-123910-4

1. Portrait painting – Technique.   I. Title.   II. Series.

ND1302.S55 1994   751.45'42   C93-095554-4

Colour reproduction by Colourscan in Singapore

Printed and bound by Graphicom in Italy

CONTENTS

INTRODUCTION

FOR MANY PAINTERS, there is no more challenging task than to come face to face with another human being and attempt to make a representation that captures something of the spirit and physical likeness of that person. Making images of ourselves is part of our basic human nature; in all cultures and from earliest times we find evidence of a fundamental urge to represent what we are and how we look. If you are relatively new to painting, you may find the idea of producing an oil portrait intimidating. But it becomes easier once you realize that the person you see in the mirror or facing you across the studio is never exactly the same as the image on the canvas. In many respects, especially technically, painting portraits can be just as straightforward as any other area of painting.

Ancient images

From the early cave paintings in France and Spain, and from the ancient civilizations of Mexico, Peru, and West Africa, there are remarkable examples of human beings coming to terms with themselves through the creation of powerful, perceptive images of the human face. Many of the images that have survived are in the form of sculpture, but there are powerful painted images on 4,000-year-old Egyptian wall paintings and in the vivid Romano-Egyptian tomb portraits painted about 1,800 years ago.

Wax Portrait of a Young Man, **late 2nd century** A.D. *15 x 8¼ in (38 x 21 cm)*
In this Romano-Egyptian mummy portrait, the youth gazes at us with a clear, calm look. The encaustic technique, involving the mixing and application of pigments in melted beeswax, gives the work an immediacy that belies its age.

Egyptian Drawing Board, *c.*1502-1450 B.C. *14 in (35.4 cm) high*
In this Egyptian drawing on a wooden board, a careful geometric system of delineating shape and form can be clearly seen. The approach is entirely linear, yet a real sense of the three-dimensional form emerges in the figure. The use of a grid, marked in a different color than the drawing, could enable the outline drawing to be transferred to a wall.

Child's drawing
This child's drawing has a simple exuberance and a delight in character that can often be lacking in the serious works of adult portrait painters.

Spontaneous expression

Images made by young children of their family and friends seem to capture immediately the warmth and complexity of their feelings, in addition to revealing the character and likeness of their subjects. Children often seem able to express themselves visually without any self-consciousness.

Although many adults lose touch with this spontaneous expression, it is within us all, and it can be retrieved. Artists who work from life know that there is an inevitable concentration and a seriousness about the process of making a portrait that separates it from other areas of painting and seems to lock into a deep part of our nature. There is a mutuality about the process that invariably establishes a deep bond between artist and sitter.

Practical approaches

In this book, we discuss the materials and skills you might need to make portraits in oils, and we outline the stages by which you can proceed to an understanding of the various technical and interpretative approaches to the subject. Projects by a number of artists demonstrate a range of different ways to make portrait images in oils. Portraits by well-known artists are also included, illustrating important aspects of portraiture, such as composition, setting, mood, and tone.

Drawings by very young children often have an astonishing intensity and a remarkable presence.

Charcoal portrait
This charcoal drawing by an eleven-year-old child reveals an acute sense of observation and strength. Each line has been made in one movement, without any erasing and starting again, and the character of the sitter comes through with clarity and force. Great conviction is required to create such a vivid image.

Ghislaine Howard, *Portrait of Jessie* 24 x 34 in (64 x 86 cm)
The world of the child is seen through adult eyes in this carefully considered commissioned portrait of a two-year-old girl. The subject is the daughter of a friend of the artist, and genuine affection for the child comes through the work, without sentimentality. A link with the family is established in the use of a backdrop that refers to the rugs made by the girl's mother; the simple geometric shapes also make associations with children's building blocks or bricks. There is a consistency in the artist's choice of palette, with its blues, oranges, and ochres, that draws together all the aspects of the composition.

A BRIEF HISTORY

PORTRAIT PAINTING IN OILS began in the fifteenth century in the Netherlands, and oil-based paint was quickly favored over egg tempera as the principal medium for portraiture. The slow-drying qualities of oil paint allowed further manipulation and blending once it had been applied to the surface of the canvas, while the translucence and resonance of oil color offered a greater range of tones and color effects than ever before. Portrait artists began to recognize that there was a new opportunity to express more accurately and vividly the special qualities of skin tones and the nuances of light and atmosphere.

Giovanni Bellini, *The Doge Leonardo Loredan*, c.1501 *24¹/₄ x 17³/₄ in (61.6 x 45.1 cm)*
Bellini's portrait is built up in layers, possibly on an egg tempera underpainting, and was made during the transitional decade from egg tempera to oil painting. The work shows all the austerity and maturity of this Venetian head of state. One senses the feeling of mutual respect between artist and sitter, which allowed Bellini to give full rein to his observational and technical skills.

JAN VAN EYCK *(c.1395-1441)* was among the great early protagonists of the oil medium for portraiture in the Netherlands. He achieved an extraordinary range of tones, with the deepest of shadows in transparent glaze colors and the clarity of bright light in opaque colors. In Italy, at the close of the fifteenth and in the early sixteenth centuries, artists such as Giovanni Bellini *(c.1435-1516)*, Raphael *(1483-1520)*, and Leonardo da Vinci *(1452-1519)* adopted and mastered the oil medium, incorporating it into their unique styles of portrait painting.

One of the most remarkable painters of this period was Albrecht Dürer *(1471-1528)*, whose oil portraits, painted in a thin, linear style, have a quality of observation that is genuinely timeless. As the sixteenth century progressed in Italy, there was a great liberation of style in the work of artists such as Titian *(c.1487-1576)* and Veronese *(c.1528-88)*. Their bold confidence with oils gives their subjects a heightened realism.

Sofonisba Anguiscola, *Portrait of the Artist's Sister in Nun's Clothing*, c.late 16th century
26 x 20¹/₂ in (66 x 52 cm)
Sofonisba Anguiscola was one of the first female painters of the Renaissance to achieve success and acclaim in her own day. The warm colors in this portrait help create a sense of true affection.

Thomas Gainsborough, *Mr. and Mrs. Andrews*, c.1750 *27¹/₂ x 47 in (69.8 x 119.4 cm)*
Gainsborough was one of the most successful society portrait painters of the eighteenth century. Here, he presents the assured young landowners in the midst of the rich farmland that sustains them.

Toulouse-Lautrec, *André Rivoire*,
1901 *21³/₄ x 18 in (55.2 x 46 cm)*
An economical approach to oil portraiture is evident in this work. The face emerges from a sketched background with warm touches of opaque color over a thin underpainting.

Gwen John, *Self-Portrait*,
***c.*1900** *24 x 15 in (61 x 38 cm)*
Gwen John, who died in 1939, had only one exhibition of work in her lifetime and remained a relatively obscure figure until recent times. This self-portrait has an expression and a demeanor, with hand on hip and arched back, which is both candid and proud in its self-possession. The head is clear against a simple background, and the dress, with its high neck, bold bow tie, and full sleeves, adds to a sense of defiance. The artist uses a predominantly opaque technique, with adjacent touches of premixed tints in low-key colors.

A new confidence

Nowhere was the new confidence and vigor more visible than in the portraits of Velázquez *(1599-1660)*, the seventeenth-century Spanish painter. His brushwork is not secondary to the image he is trying to create, but autonomous, allowing the characters in his portraits to emerge with a spell-binding immediacy. In the Netherlands, Frans Hals *(c.1583-1666)* was working in a similar way, using lively brushwork to produce portraits with an engaging presence.

The history of oil portraits is a history of changing techniques and approaches. The imprimatura or toned ground, for example, was used extensively up to the mid-to-late nineteenth century. For artists such as Rubens *(1577-1640)*, Rembrandt *(1606-69)*, and van Dyck *(1599-1641)*, working in the seventeenth century, the mid-toned ground provided a unifying matrix underlying the brushstrokes, allowing an economy in the painting style that could not be created with a white ground.

Changing styles

In the eighteenth century, the great English portrait painter Thomas Gainsborough *(1727-88)* used thin washes of diluted oil color in a fluent technique that has left many well-preserved and technically sound portraits. His contemporary, Joshua Reynolds *(1723-92)*, experimented with unstable materials such as bitumen, and his works have suffered as a result.

Late nineteenth and early twentieth-century developments led to an explosion of stylistic diversity in portraiture, ranging from the unparalleled intensity of color and expression in van Gogh's *(1853-90)* portraits, to the more monochromatic Cubist remodeling of the human head by Picasso *(1881-1973)* and Braque *(1882-1963)*. In our time, artists continue to strive to represent the truth of what they see.

Craigie Aitchison, RA, *Portrait of Naaotwa*
***Swayne*, 1988** *24 x 20 in (61 x 50.8 cm)*
Aitchison's painting is characterized by the use of flat, strong color, brushed thinly onto the canvas so that it seems to become part of the canvas itself. This portrait has been pared down to the absolute essentials.

OIL COLORS

Azurite and pigment

Recommended colors

Permanent Rose (T)
(Quinacridone Red)

Cadmium Red (O)

Cadmium Yellow Pale (O)

Winsor Green (T)
(Phthalocyanine Green)

Winsor Blue (T)
(Phthalocyanine Blue)

Titanium White (O)

Yellow Ochre (O)

Burnt Sienna (T)

OIL PAINTS ARE MADE by grinding pigments with a vegetable oil such as linseed, safflower, or poppy oil. The oil gives the paint its characteristic appearance and distinctive buttery texture. Pigments ground in oil have a particular depth and resonance of color because of the amount of light the oil absorbs and reflects. Apart from providing this unique color quality, the drying oils also protect the pigment particles and act as an adhesive in attaching the pigment to the ground. Oil paints can be opaque, such as Titanium White, or transparent, such as Winsor Blue. Opaque colors generally obliterate the color they are painted over, while transparent colors can be applied in thin translucent films over dried colors for glazing and other effects.

Cadmium Red pigment

Yellow Ochre pigment

Recommended colors for portrait painting

The following opaque (O), transparent (T), and semi-transparent (ST) colors are recommended: Cadmium Red (O) or Winsor Red (O), Permanent Rose (T) or Alizarin Crimson (T), Indian Red (O), Cadmium Yellow Pale (O), Cadmium Lemon (O), Winsor Yellow (ST), Winsor Lemon (ST), Lemon Yellow Hue (O), Transparent Gold Ochre (T), Winsor Blue (T), Cobalt Blue (ST), Ultramarine Blue (ST) or Cerulean Blue (ST), Dioxazine Violet (T), Quinacridone Violet (T), Cobalt Violet (ST), Winsor Green (T) or Viridian (T), Oxide of Chromium Green (O), Terre Verte (T), Titanium White (O), Flake White (O), Yellow Ochre (O), Raw Sienna (T), Raw Umber (T), Burnt Umber (T) or Burnt Sienna (T).

Pigments
Originally derived from earths, minerals, and vegetables, many pigments are now synthetic.

Mixing colors
In portrait painting, opaque colors are often used for light areas and transparent colors for dark areas. You can add a little white to a transparent color to make it opaque. If, for example, you add a touch of Titanium White to transparent Winsor Blue, you will get an opaque blue. If you mix two transparent colors, such as Permanent Rose and Winsor Blue, you will make a deep, transparent color.

DILUTING PAINTS

You will need to use distilled turpentine as a solvent to dilute your paints. You can mix solvent with stand oil (a thickened form of linseed oil) to make a painting or glazing medium, or you can buy oil painting medium, which is a mixture of the two. Be careful with solvents. Always use a screw-top dipper and replace the lid after dipping in the brush. If you are painting large areas using oil color thinned with a lot of solvent, you should use an organic solvent mask to minimize health risks.

Stand oil   *Oil painting medium*   *Solvent*

Premixing colors

The preparation on your palette of a range of premixed colors for flesh tones is a very sensible practice. It enables you to model the face with the same range of colors throughout at least one stage of painting, without having constantly to remix. Once the face has been modeled, the colors can be adjusted.

Study in four flesh tones

Here, four flesh tones have been premixed from Burnt Sienna, Titanium White, Cadmium Red, and Yellow Ochre and applied to establish the main areas of tone and color in an oil portrait. The visible joins between the colors can then be blended into an imperceptible fusion of tones by brushing across the join with a clean dry brush.

Opaque tints and transparent darks

Mix opaque tints and transparent darks from the recommended palette **(1)** of Permanent Rose, Cadmium Red, Cadmium Yellow Pale, Yellow Ochre, Winsor Green, Winsor Blue, and Burnt Sienna. The premixed opaque tints **(2)** are browns (BS, TW), pinks (CR, TW), pink-yellows (CR, TW, YO), warm pink-yellow-browns (YO, TW, BS) and cool pink-yellow-browns (YO, TW, BS, WB), greens (WG, BS, TW), and blues (WB, TW, BS). The transparent darks **(3)** are mixed from Permanent Rose, Burnt Sienna, Winsor Blue, and Winsor Green.

BRUSHES & BRUSHWORK

YOUR MOST IMPORTANT TOOLS are your brushes, and how your portrait looks depends greatly on their quality. There are two main types of brush: stiff-hair brushes, known as bristle or hog brushes, and soft-hair or sable brushes. Both types are also available made from synthetic fibers. Round, flat, and filbert bristle brushes are commonly used in portrait work, because they are very good for moving paint around large areas of the textured canvas surface. Soft-hair brushes are used for more delicate manipulations and for work on a small scale. Oil painting brushes traditionally have long handles, which allow the artist to work at some distance from the painting and see how it is developing as a whole.

Store your brushes upright

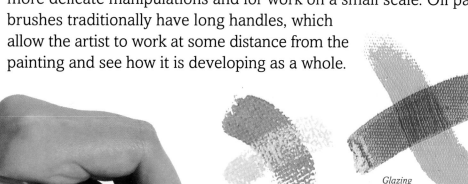

Glazing

Scumbling

Glazing
Glazing is the application of a thin film of translucent color, mixed with a little oil painting medium, over another dried layer of paint. The color below remains visible but has been modified by the glaze applied over it.

Scumbling and dry brush
Scumbling is brushing one color loosely over another dried color so that the color below shows through in places. In dry-brush work, you stroke stiff paint over the painted canvas so that the raised or textured areas of the canvas pick up the paint while the original color shows in the troughs or indentations.

No. 3 round bristle brush

No. 8 short flat bristle brush

Palette knife

Round bristle brushes
Round bristle brushes have a good paint-holding capacity. Use them to make full strokes with thick oil color or for dry-brush effects.

Flat bristle brushes
Flat bristle brushes make square-shaped strokes. These are often left unblended to give a direct, chunky look to an image.

Painting knives
Painting knives are used to apply or remove and manipulate thick oil color. You can also use them for scraped effects, known as sgraffito.

Fine, delicate strokes

Painting detail
Use a round soft-hair brush for applying touches of color within small areas. The point of a small round sable or nylon brush can be used to paint the most difficult shapes. In a portrait, much of the detailed work on the features is done with a thin round sable brush, such as a No. 2 (*see* pp. 60-61).

No. 2 round sable brush

Impasted brushwork

Impasto
Use a large filbert bristle brush to make broad, impasted strokes, using thick paint either straight from the tube or loosely mixed. If you use a filbert, the start of the stroke will have the characteristic rounded look that many painters prefer to the harder square strokes of a flat brush (*see* pp. 32-33).

No. 10 filbert bristle brush

Strokes of thin color

Thin color
A small filbert is ideal for the application of a series of thin adjacent colors onto a white ground. The strokes retain their purity of color and are given a characteristic and recognizable texture where the relatively coarse bristles scratch through the thin paint to the primer or color beneath (*see* pp. 44-47).

No. 4 filbert bristle brush

Unblended, adjacent tints

Broken color
Here, a medium-sized round bristle brush has been used to apply adjacent touches of opaque, unblended color over a dark ground. The round brush allows the artist to apply enough thick, rich tints to sustain the intensity of color over the ground, while carefully controlling how much paint is applied (*see* pp. 34-37).

No. 6 round bristle brush

Finely blended brushwork

Fine blending
Clean brushes slightly dampened in solvent are used to blend adjacent colors or tones so that the eye moves imperceptibly from one color to the next (*see* pp. 52-55).

SUPPORTS & GROUNDS

YOU CAN PAINT on a rigid support, such as a board or panel, or on a flexible support, such as canvas. Oak, poplar, and mahogany panels provide stable support, though it is more common for artists to use plywood, hardboard, and fiberboard panels. Unless you are painting on a small scale, it is easier to paint portraits on canvases, because they are lighter and more portable. The traditional choice is linen canvas, made from flax fibers that are long and strong, but high-quality heavyweight cotton canvases are also available. Whichever support you choose, each will have its own characteristic feel, depending on the ground or primer applied. A primer or ground is a layer of paint used to seal the support and separate it from the oil color. You can size and prime your own supports or buy them already prepared.

A sturdy easel will allow you to work vigorously without fear of the canvas moving around.

Recommended sizes
Choose the size of support to suit your portrait format. Sizes are not prescribed, but you may try those shown above.

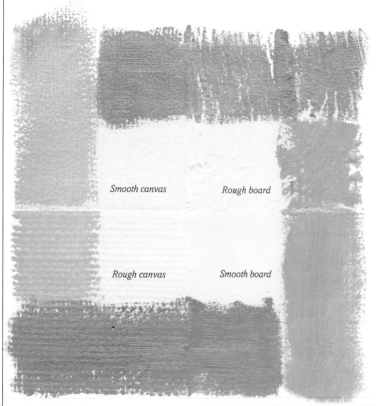

Smooth canvas   *Rough board*

Rough canvas   *Smooth board*

Rough and smooth grounds
On a smooth ground, such as a primed fine linen or a smooth panel, you can see every mark you make with great clarity. This is ideal for the modeling and blending of fine detail or for making loose, sweeping brushstrokes. A rough surface, such as a coarse-grained canvas, will break up the brushstroke and give it a pitted or textured appearance. Thus, a craggy, chunky image can be economically produced.

Plywood   *Hardboard*   *Medium-density fiberboard*

Fine linen   *Coarse linen*   *Cotton duck 12oz*

Choosing a support
The texture of a linen canvas is dictated by the method of spinning the fiber and by its thickness or weight. A coarse canvas will give a good key to the paint and will provide a texture that has a significant impact on the way the painting looks. A smooth fine-grade linen is particularly suitable for highly detailed work. Cotton duck canvas is pleasant to use, but choose one of the heavier weights, preferably a 12-oz or 15-oz one. Hardboard, plywood, and medium-density fiberboard make good rigid supports, but only in small sizes; otherwise you will have to glue them to a rigid frame to prevent them from warping. Size and prime both sides of the panels to retain stability.

Stretching a canvas

When you attach your canvas to the stretcher frame, your aim is to make it as taut as possible, with an even tension throughout the canvas and without puckers or ridge lines. Stretcher pieces are available at most art-supply stores or from framing stores. To reduce the strain imposed on the fabric, it is best to use stretchers with rounded edges.

1 ▲ Assemble the four sides of your stretcher frame, using a rubber hammer to tap them together. Make sure the frame is square by using a set square or by checking that the diagonal measurements are exactly the same.

2 ▲ Lay the frame over a large piece of canvas and cut around it, allowing a margin of about 3 in (7-8 cm) on all sides to pull the canvas over the stretcher frame.

3 ▲ Pull the canvas over the stretcher frame by hand or use canvas pliers. Staple or tack the canvas down in stages (see diagram below), with two or three evenly spaced staples at each stage.

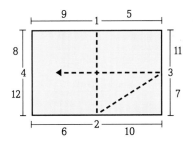

Staple the canvas in a specific order

4 ▲ Make two folds in the canvas at each corner, pull one fold over the other, and staple them to the frame. This will help maintain an even tension across the canvas.

5 ▲ Tap a wedge into each corner of the frame. These wedges are known as stretcher keys, and they will help keep the canvas as taut as possible.

Sizing and priming

To size a canvas, apply one coat of warm size, made with 1 oz (25-30 grams) per 4 c (1 litre) of water, and allow it to dry. For sizing panels, apply one coat of glue size, made with 2¹/₂ oz (70 grams) per 4 c (1 litre) of water, and allow it to dry. Prime both canvases and panels with two coats of commercial oil painting primer or a white oil-based undercoat for gloss paint. It is also possible to prime a rigid panel with an acrylic or PVA emulsion, such as an acrylic gesso primer.

1 ▲ Stir the size into the water and heat in a double boiler (or a pot with a saucepan) to avoid overheating. When the size has dissolved, apply it to the canvas with a large brush while it is still hot. This allows the size to penetrate the fibers of the canvas.

2 ▲ Allow the size to dry thoroughly before adding the primer. Use a large brush to apply oil painting primer or oil-based undercoat for white gloss paint. Apply the second coat by brushing at right angles to the first.

PRELIMINARY SKETCHING

ONE OF THE most important foundations of good portrait work is sketching. Among the best sketches are those made rapidly on a very small scale. It is a good idea to get into the habit of taking a sketchbook with you when you go to concerts or restaurants, or when you travel by train or go on vacation. Make studies of the characters you see around you, sketching people of different ages and nationalities. At home, make drawings of your own family while they are watching television or sleeping. It is best to draw people who are a fair distance away – about eight to twelve feet. This has two advantages. First, you will not be disturbing your subject as you draw. Second, you won't be troubled by too much detail and so will be able to see the whole shape of the head and features clearly. This will help you sharpen your powers of observation and will be invaluable when you work more formally with a sitter.

Drawing from life
Arrange to draw your family and friends from life, and make several small-scale studies. Working with charcoal, conté crayon, or pencil may help you relax with your drawing in a way that you might not yet feel able to do with brush and paint. Studies in pen and wash or watercolor are also very helpful preliminary stages to painting directly with oil color on canvas.

Conté crayons
Conté crayons make strong, broad marks and give a lively, loose feel to a study. A round graphite stick is also ideal for more vigorous sketching.

Round graphite stick

Sketchbooks
Sketchbooks invariably contain an assortment of images and words. Use your sketchbook as a diary of the people you see, drawing heads and faces from all angles. Make simple line drawings, letting the pencil or pen follow the profile or the shape of the head and features. Try to do this directly, without going over the same line twice or having to erase the line and try again.

Pencils

Pencil marks can be simply erased and redrawn, making this the most versatile of sketching tools. The crisp, dry lines of a hard pencil allow sensitive detail, while a softer pencil will make dense, velvety marks similar to those of a crayon. In this drawing (*right*), the lines follow the contours of the old man's temples, cheeks, hair, and beard with an easy fluency.

Pen

Pencil

Pen and wash

Working directly with pen and wash enables you to make a fresh, direct statement with no erasing. Your study may not be strictly accurate, but the briefest outlines can convey a subject's character.

Tonal studies

When you come to paint an oil portrait, you will find it useful to make a number of small preparatory studies to enable you to find out just how you want your sitter to look in the painting. It is worth spending time on a tonal study. In this charcoal drawing (*right*), the tones are very well developed. The darker areas around the right side of the head lend warmth and sympathy to the subject's expression, while a series of emphatic marks around the ear, nostril, eyelids, and neckline gives the image a great deal of vigor.

Charcoal

The strong black mark of charcoal allows you to make bold tonal studies very quickly. Use your fingers for blending and an eraser for bright highlights. Used tonally, charcoal brings out the texture of the paper very well.

Charcoal

17

TRANSFERRING AN IMAGE

S OME PORTRAIT PAINTERS PREFER to go through a number of preliminary stages before committing to canvas, and such stages often take the form of preparatory sketches and photographs. When you come to transfer the image onto canvas, you can do so freehand, but you may not find this accurate enough, particularly if you are working from a photograph. Specialized technical equipment, such as an epidiascope, an enlarger, or a slide projector, will enable you to enlarge the contours of the face directly onto the canvas. If you do not have access to such equipment, you can use the time-honored method of transferring an image by using a grid system.

L-shaped viewers made from cardboard

Capturing an image

Photographs are a popular source of reference for portrait painting. Use your camera to record a series of poses, looking from the right or left, up or down, and trying full-face, three-quarter, or profile views. Experiment with different lights, remembering that it is often better to use an image that has been taken out of the direct sunlight, where the shadows are less harsh.

L-shaped viewers can be made quickly and easily; just cut out two right angles from thick, dark cardboard.

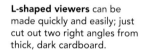

Using L-shaped viewers

Once you have chosen the image best suited to your proposed portrait, use L-shaped viewers to decide how much of the photograph you want to use in your painting. You can, of course, lose any extraneous detail or change the format by shading out the areas you wish to exclude with a pen. Here, the focus of the work is the head and shoulders of the girl – this is the area that will be squared up and transferred to the canvas.

Decide which elements of the image to include in your portrait.

Squaring up the image

You can square up directly onto the photo itself, using a fine line pen and a set square. Use a scale of square that will allow you to transfer the broad areas, as well as any detail that you think relevant. Here, the features are squared up in smaller-scale squares than those used for the main outline of the head. This allows you to be more accurate when you draw in the features. Mark an identical but larger-scale grid on your canvas and work from square to square, drawing in the main details.

Protect your sketch by using a layer of acetate for marking the lines of the grid.

The grid has been marked directly onto the pencil sketch with well-spaced squares.

Transferring a sketch

You can transfer a sketch or study in a similar way. You may not mind marking a grid on the drawing itself, but if you want to protect the sketch, then square up a piece of thin acetate and superimpose it over the drawing. Here, the aim is to transfer only the broad outline of the profile.

OTHER REFERENCES

● Some artists combine sittings from life with photographs. If you have slides, there are commercially available electric viewers that allow you to refer to your slide in daylight while painting. The painting below is so large that it has been stretched on the studio wall during painting.

● There are now compact disc players that allow you to refer to a still photo on a television screen for as long as necessary. Your photographic dealer will transfer your prints to compact disc format for you.

GALLERY OF STUDIES

FOR MANY ARTISTS, preparatory studies are an indispensable stage in the process of making an oil portrait. They provide an opportunity to capture something of the mood or character you wish to develop in the painting. Such studies range from tiny, rapid pencil sketches to large-scale, fully modeled studies, and they often have a freshness that is lacking in the finished painting. Here, the versatility of pencil is revealed in the crisp, graphic lines of Picasso's drawing and the intensely worked study by Neale Worley. The powerful tonal range of charcoal and Conté crayon is clear, as is the mood of spontaneity created by energetic pen and wash work.

Pablo Picasso, *Portrait of Paloma,* 1952 *26 x 20 in (66 x 51 cm)*
Picasso's vigorous drawing has a childlike quality that echoes the youthfulness of the sitter. He has simplified and exaggerated the forms to give the drawing an almost diagrammatic appearance. In doing so, he has captured a real sense of the child's character. She has a clear-eyed, bright, and alert look, with an open, untroubled expression.

Rembrandt, *A Young Woman Seated in an Armchair,* c.1654-60 *6¹/₂ x 5³/₄ in (16.3 x 14.3 cm)*
This pen and wash study is a work of quite exceptional intimacy and power, one in which Rembrandt has managed to convey a genuine sense of the moment. There is an edginess about the way the woman leans forward as if about to stand up. Her hands are clasped tightly, held against her stomach, and her face is cast down. She is entirely self-contained.

This detail of the woman's face shows an exposed, sensitive expression, which leads us to speculate on the circumstances surrounding the drawing.

Polly Lister, *Elizabeth*

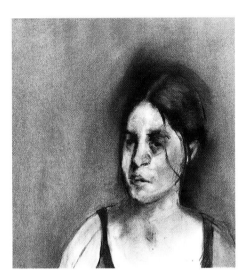

12¹/₂ x 12¹/₄ in (32 x 31 cm)
This study has the kind of
immediacy that charcoal
can bring to a drawing,
with its rubbed halftones,
areas of velvety shadow,
and highlights picked out
with an eraser. The subject's
face emerges softly from the
gray ground. She seems to
be turning half away from
the artist and her eyes do
not quite connect with
the viewer's. This slight
sense of unease gives the
drawing its authenticity.

Mandy Lindsay, *Standing
Figure* 57 x 20 in (146 x 51 cm)
This full-length study demonstrates how
charcoal and Conté crayon can be used
to give a strong tonal rendering to a
preliminary study. The drawing shows
a complete range of tones from deep
shadow to bright highlight, with all
the folds in the clothes fully modeled.
It is extremely useful to have this kind
of study as a guide when painting.

Neale Worley, *Lord Pennock*
22 x 18 in (56 x 46 cm)
Neale Worley's pencil drawing
is the most rigorously worked
and fully resolved of these
studies. The effect of so highly
representational an approach
is to allow the character and
maturity of the sitter to come
through with genuine sensitivity
and compassion.

THE HEAD

WHEN AS CHILDREN we draw heads, we invariably make a circle and place the eyes, nose, and mouth in the middle. We are, of course, most familiar with this direct, full-face view, because it is the one we see in the mirror. But a portrait artist needs to be aware of the shape of the head viewed from different angles, and how this shape varies, often dramatically, from person to person. Certainly, it is helpful to study the anatomy of the human head, but it may be more practical and useful to make a series of drawings and painted studies concentrating on the basic planes of the head and on the way features change in appearance as one's viewpoint changes.

Measuring with a pencil
When you are drawing, it may be useful to hold a pencil at arm's length and slide your thumb up and down it to measure the relative distances between features.

Full-face study

Three-quarter view (right)

Profile study

Back view

Monochromatic oil sketches
For painting monochromatic studies of the head from all angles, use a model with short hair. This will help you to see the changing shape of the head clearly. Lightly sketch the outlines in charcoal before using a small sable brush and thin transparent color to draw in the features. Use a bristle brush with thin Burnt Sienna oil color to sketch in the main tonal areas.

Eye studies
Concentrating on one particular feature, such as the eye, will add a degree of objectivity to your perception and help you see parts of the face in a completely fresh way. Use watercolor, pen and wash, or pencil to make a series of careful studies, viewing the eye from the side, three-quarters, and full-face left and right.

Three-quarter view (left)

Simple light effects
A series of charcoal studies will help you understand how light modifies the appearance of facial features. Here, bright light from the right throws the side of the face into sharp relief and highlights the contours of the temples, cheek, and chin.

Unusual effects
Sometimes light can cast strange shadows, for example, when foliage shields the face from direct sunlight. Here, strong light spots the face unevenly, creating sharp highlights on the bridge of the nose, the chin, forehead, and neck.

A powerful medium such as charcoal is ideal for making studies of light effects.

STUDYING FEATURES

● Making closely observed oil studies of individual features gives you the opportunity to look at them quite separately from the head as a whole. Since you do not need to be concerned about getting a recognizable likeness of the face, you can relax and really examine the shapes and forms of each feature.

● You can experiment by taking photocopies of your studies and making montages, with the eyes close together or wide apart, for example, and in various configurations. Such exercises can teach us a great deal about the way we read people's faces.

Light from below
Bright light from a source below the head exaggerates the shadows and creates striking, rugged effects.

CAPTURING A LIKENESS

Compare your sketches and studies with a snapshot to see if you have captured a good likeness.

MAKING A PORTRAIT RECOGNIZABLE is a complex task. What you see may not coincide with how your sitters see themselves or how others view them. Of course, we can use the grid system, photography, or projection to help us accurately lay down the relative position of the features on the canvas. But whether or not the image has that indefinable quality that makes the character shine through the image is ultimately a result of the observation of the artist, the tractability of the materials, and the particular chemistry of each painting session. If you need a model so you can practice getting a good likeness, use yourself. A self-portrait allows you to look closely at head structure and the shapes of features without embarrassment.

A broad likeness
Half close your eyes to get a blurred image in the mirror and make a charcoal drawing. Losing the details in this way will help you concentrate on the shape of the face and get a broad likeness.

Diagrammatic profile sketch in pencil

Tonal profile study in charcoal

Profile studies
Set up mirrors so you can see your own profile and plot an accurate image in pencil. Make a tonal version in charcoal or crayon.

Color and tone
Make a series of oil studies in which you try to correlate what you see in terms of color and tone with the marks you make on the canvas. Slightly exaggerate each separate area of tone and color to build up a patchwork of unblended brushstrokes that map out the planes and features of the face in relation to the highlights, middle tones, and shadows. Juxtapose cool hues with warm ones so there is a lively pattern of color in addition to an accuracy of tone. If you check your reflection frequently, and work boldly from what you see, you will be surprised how quickly a likeness begins to emerge.

In this dark full-face study, the eyes look at us candidly.

Placing and scaling features

Make a series of careful pencil drawings in which you try to place and scale the features accurately in relation to each other. Draw lines as guides to the relative distances between features. The distance between the eyes is particularly crucial to the accuracy of a full-face image.

Adjusting your pose

Notice how your features change their shape when you adjust your pose slightly. Hold your head up, and your forehead and nose appear shorter, with the cheeks and chin dominating the image. If you look down, your nose and forehead appear longer. For unusual poses, incorporating tone can help you make more sense of the forms.

William Wood

The yellows have been emphasized in this solid, wide-faced portrait.

Warm pinks accentuate the lean, exposed look of this study.

25

SELF-PORTRAIT STUDY

A screw-top dipper provides easy access to a small amount of solvent.

THE SELF-PORTRAIT allows a closer observation of your subject than you might get with a sitter, often resulting in an unblinking intensity unusual in other kinds of portraiture. This rapidly made study is painted on a white ground, which keeps the colors fresh and reinforces the rather "exposed" look. The colors are relatively low-key, with the cool blue-grays complementing the warm orange-browns, while tonal contrasts are used to good effect with the pale face framed by the dark hair. The painterly integration of hair with background also helps push the face forward. By these means, our attention is focused on the face and its unresolved, somewhat nervous expression reflected in the flickering brushwork.

1 ◄ Set up a mirror and study your face carefully before beginning to sketch out the lines of your eyes and nose. Working outward from the eyes, methodically stroke in each line with a small sable brush. Close observation and accurate measuring at this stage will help you achieve a real likeness as the study progresses. Suggest the areas of tone around the eyes and nose with a small flat bristle brush.

2 ◄ Using a small sable brush, paint the outlines of the lips. They will immediately enliven the canvas, making a bold statement that will require little additional work. Check your reflection to assess the distances between features; how, for instance, the corners of the mouth align with the eyes, and what the distance is between the tip of the nose and the upper lip.

3 ▶ Once the shapes and measurements of the features have been established, add the line of the chin and begin loosely to suggest the hair. Use a large filbert bristle brush to build up texture rapidly, painting strong brushstrokes of blues, purples, and browns.

4 ▶ Now pay attention to the pale flesh tones, using a medium-sized flat bristle brush to blend wet-in-wet with gentle, flickering brushwork. Gradually thicken your paint mixes to create a sense of solid flesh. Switch to a small sable brush for the warm pink shadows at the sides of the nose and on the cheeks.

5 ▶ Pick out final details, such as eyelashes, and strengthen the lines of the eyes with a small sable brush. The gaze is direct and honest, intensified by the strong tones of the eyelids and brows. Finally, tone down the hair with a medium-sized flat bristle brush.

Self-Portrait study

The finished study has a stronger sense of immediacy and honesty than a more highly worked painting. The visible brushstrokes contribute to an unfinished, scrubbed background effect, which helps further dramatize the impact of the face itself.

The low-key browns and blue-grays of the hair are integrated with the gray background, pushing forward the face with its warmer tones and thicker paint effects.

The strong line of the mouth forms a triangle of dark tone with the bold lines of the eyes and eyebrows.

The cool blue-grays of the clothes are reflected in the irises of the eyes and the shadows around the nose, accentuating the use of a limited range of colors in the study.

Sue Sareen

Materials

No. 2 round sable brush

No. 1 short flat bristle brush

No. 5 short flat bristle brush

No. 8 long filbert bristle brush

27

GALLERY OF SELF-PORTRAITS

IN THE BEST SELF-PORTRAITS there is a truth and directness that allow the character of the artist to be present in a quite intimate way. This element of self-exposure can be overplayed, but in these works there is a sense of restraint that lends dignity to the images. The tone and treatment vary dramatically, from the bright clarity and poise of the Vigée-Lebrun to the darker, low-key treatment of Tai-Shan Schierenberg's portrait, which pushes toward us with an almost physical presence. Philip Sutton's painting has the gravity that comes from a more mature artist, while Christopher Prewett's has the edginess of a young painter.

Elisabeth Vigée-Lebrun, *Self-Portrait,* **1791** *39 x 31³/₄ in (99 x 80.5 cm) This self-portrait has a wonderfully fresh and open quality. The atmosphere is light, faintly self-mocking, and full of enjoyment. The artist has taken great care over her choice of costume; the white turban and collar frame the face, with its clear eyes and direct expression, and contrast with the black dress. Cool background colors complement the warm flesh tones and the bold red sash, reinforcing the sense of poise and balance in the work.*

Philip Sutton, RA, *The King,* **1991** *36 x 36 in (91.5 x 91.5 cm) Philip Sutton's self-portrait is one in a series in which he assumes different roles associated with the particular costume or headgear he is wearing. The costume is a device which liberates a mood or feeling within the artist's own character. It is an outward means whereby the artist can come to know and represent his inner feelings. Here, the crown evokes both king and clown or fool, and the bright colors of the crown are in opposition to the careworn, resigned look in the eyes. The rather diagrammatic method of painting, together with the cool, atmospheric blue, adds to a feeling of desolation.*

Tai-Shan Schierenberg, *Self-Portrait*
Small Head *9 x 6 in (23 x 15.3 cm)*
This is an example of the kind of rapidly made alla prima self-portrait that ruggedly sketches out the broad structure of the face and gives one a real sense of the artist's presence. The paint is used with an impasted consistency throughout the work, and there is a boldness in the decision making and a lack of fussiness which gives the portrait its impact. A color harmony of subtle low-key mixtures is used, and the cool background brings forward the warmer colors in the face. A strong use of tone shows the deep shadows in a face lit from above.

In this detail, the bold, vigorous brushstrokes have been made with a flat bristle brush. When a color is overlaid wet-in-wet, as with the shadows below the cheekbone, the paint has a striated appearance where the two colors mix loosely together. Such additions of color have to be boldly applied, otherwise a muddy effect can result.

Christopher Prewett,
Self-Portrait, *46 x 35³/₄ in (117 x 91 cm)*
This is a strong self-portrait which has, at first sight, a rather confrontational quality. It is, in fact, an extremely sensitive work, in which we can follow the artist's efforts to come to terms with himself. This is clear in the way the brushstrokes flicker and move in an enquiring, nervous manner around the forms. The strong triangles of the arms and hands, solid on the hips, hold together an image constantly on the move.

A limited color range in the flesh tones of this detail gives a resolved feel to the head as a whole.

The eyes fix the viewer with a firm, candid look. They provide an area of sharp focus against a backdrop of shifting brushstrokes.

COLORED GROUNDS

THE ADVANTAGE OF WORKING on a white ground is that the white illuminates the paints in their true colors. However, there are very good reasons for painting a portrait on a toned or colored ground. With a mid-toned ground, for example, you can use the ground color as an intermediate tone between the lights and darks. This allows you to sketch in a well-modeled image very economically, using opaque mixes with white for the light tones, and thin transparent dark colors for the darks. There are two main types of colored ground: the toned ground, which is an opaque color either incorporated into the primer or painted over it, and the "imprimatura," which is a thin layer of translucent color laid over the white primer.

Study on a dark ground
If you work on a dark ground, you can use opaque colors to bring out the areas of the face that catch the light. This is an effective way of modeling images out of the shadows. Here, the contours of the eye are sketched in and will be built up until enough definition has been achieved.

COLORING A GROUND

● For an opaque ground, mix the chosen color with white primer or white oil color and paint it evenly over the canvas. Allow the paint to dry thoroughly.

● For a uniformly toned imprimatura (*above*), use a wide brush to apply horizontal strokes of thinly diluted oil color. Brush lightly once again and the applied color will settle to give an even appearance.

● For an imprimatura with variegated tone (*above*), mix the oil color with turpentine to a fairly thin consistency and apply it with vigorous brushstrokes at various angles onto the canvas.

Choosing a colored ground
Historically, it has been popular to underpaint flesh tones in Terre Verte, a natural green earth color. The green can still be discerned in the shadows and acts as a complementary color to the opaque warm flesh tones painted over it. In the preliminary stages for this portrait, the shape of the head and hands are given a similar toned ground using Oxide of Chromium Green, while the rest of the image, which is going to be predominantly in shadow, has been prepared with a warm Burnt Sienna imprimatura.

The transparent ground provides a warm background color for the cool thin glazes that will be used for the deep tones of the costume.

Preliminary modeling
The preliminary modeling for the hands has been achieved using white oil color in a dry-brush technique which brings out the basic form. The shadows have also been sketched in with thin Burnt Umber. The next stage is to paint the flesh tones with premixed tints.

As the white color is applied, the form of the hands quickly emerges from the green ground.

Study on toned grounds
Make experimental studies to find the best colored ground.

White ground
A white ground illuminates color and, lighter in tone than everything you paint, makes your strokes appear darker than on a toned ground.

Red ground
A strong red ground warms up the image and pushes the face forward. The contrast between the blue in the eye and the red below is particularly strong.

Green ground
A green ground gives the warm pinks of the lips a richness and body. The muted tone also subdues the browns and ochres in the hair.

Blue ground
On a dark blue ground, the color effects are more brittle. The flesh tones need to be warmed up considerably to bring color to the face.

Color effects
An opaque or transparent brushstroke will have a very different appearance on a transparent ground than on an opaque ground. The tone of the ground will also greatly affect the appearance of the overlaid color.

Opaque pink and transparent brown on a transparent Burnt Sienna ground.

Opaque pink and tranparent brown on an opaque Yellow Ochre ground.

Opaque pink and transparent brown on a transparent Burnt Umber ground.

Pink and brown on an opaque Chromium of Oxide ground.

31

BOLD COLOR EFFECTS

A preliminary study in charcoal offers the opportunity to study your subject's features and assess the tonal range.

THIS LIVELY PAINTING relies on the deep crimson imprimatura to provide an underlying ground color behind and between the brushstrokes. This has the effect of integrating the work, creating a unifying matrix of color. The red resonates with the near black, the blue-gray, and the orange-brown of the face. The image is sketched out in a strong, diagrammatic way and then worked up with bold, chunky brushstrokes. The style of painting has a deceptive simplicity. There is an underlying tonal structure that holds the work together, and the artist has avoided detail except where it is absolutely necessary. The eyes are the main focus of the face; they hold our attention, while around them the paint moves and turns. For all its boldness of style and economy of color, the work remains a sensitive portrait.

Materials

Ultramarine Blue

Titanium White

Cadmium Yellow

Alizarin Crimson

1 ▲ From a palette of four colors mix Ultramarine Blue and Alizarin Crimson to make a dark purple. Sketch in the features with a medium-sized round bristle brush.

2 ◀ Begin blocking in the background with brisk strokes of blue-grays. The wet red ground shows through, giving a richness and warmth to the cool blues. Use a large flat bristle brush for this vigorous brushwork.

3 ▶ Establish the tonal structure of the face in logical stages. First, use pale tones to suggest the fall of light on the left side of the face, then add dark orange-browns for the areas of shadow on the right side of the face. Apply broad, chunky strokes with a large filbert bristle brush.

4 ▲ Work up the skin tones to give the face shape and form before picking out the details of the features. Tint the whites of the eyes with Ultramarine Blue to reflect the background color. Use a medium-sized round bristle brush for these finer strokes.

Charcoal

No. 1 round bristle brush

No. 2 long filbert bristle brush

No. 5 round bristle brush

No. 10 long filbert bristle brush

6 ▲ Using a large flat bristle brush paint thick, creamy highlights above the eyebrows. This lively, impasted brushwork emphasizes the forehead and eyes, drawing the face forward to suggest a three-dimensional solidity.

5 ▲ Integrate the face with the background by repeating the same blue-grays in the hair and flesh tones. Such repetition of a limited range of color tints gives the portrait a close color harmony.

7 ◀ Using a small round bristle brush, add impasted yellow highlights to the nose to give it prominence. Finally, deepen the dark green shadows under the eyes, strengthening the bold rhythm of dark tone that runs through the portrait.

No. 8 short flat bristle brush

Portrait on a red ground

The finished painting suggests a man of vibrant character and intense emotion. His eyes engage the viewer with a strong determination. The carefully crafted tonal structure of the painting works with the unifying warmth of the red ground to bring real life and energy to the subject.

The subtle, unfinished appearance of the background gives the face maximum impact.

The transparent red ground glows through the blues and browns, creating bold effects with a limited palette.

Rachel Clark

PROFILE PORTRAIT

The sitter is positioned with the light source in front of him. His head is held high and the pose is strong and dramatic.

Using a black ground
On a white ground, you usually begin by painting the shadows, but on a black ground you paint in reverse and start by painting in the lights in pale, opaque colors.

BECAUSE WE RARELY SEE our own profile, the profile portrait tends to have a naked clarity and objective truth that the full-face or three-quarter view might not reveal. That sense of objectivity characterizes this portrait, painted in an opaque technique on a black ground. As the painting progresses over the course of two sessions, the image emerges from the dark ground into a rugged three-dimensionality, as the artist applies adjacent rich, warm tints of opaque color. If you look at the finished painting with half-closed eyes, you will see how the strength and completeness of the work stems from the artist's strict control of tone.

1 ▶ Draw in the brief outlines of the profile with thinned Yellow Ochre before applying the first layer of paint. Block in the hair with a well-diluted mix of Ultramarine Blue, Burnt Sienna, and Titanium White, using a small round bristle brush. The opaque black ground provides a grainy surface that is ideal for black hair, allowing you to achieve texture economically.

2 ◀ Cover the whole face and neck with thin flesh mixes, juxtaposing warm and cool tints in a wide range of tones. For dark skins, deep tints of Burnt Sienna, Permanent Rose, and Cadmium Orange with white provide rich, warm colors. Use tints of Winsor Green or Terre Verte for their cool complementary tones. A small round bristle brush, such as a No. 3, is ideal for applying deft, chunky strokes of color.

3 ▶ After painting the shirt collar and vest, scumble a pale blue over the black background with a mix of Titanium White, Ultramarine Blue, and a little Cadmium Orange. This will instantly give the profile definition. Once every area of the canvas is covered, leave the painting to dry thoroughly; that way you will avoid muddy effects later.

Halfway stage

At the end of the first session, the profile has a loose, energetic feel, and the drama of the pose is already clear. Most of the basic tonal areas are sketched in and the tonal scale established: the collar represents the lightest note and the hair the darkest. In places, the tones are either still a little flat, such as the areas around the eye and nose, or too pronounced, as in the area of the temple. This is quite normal at this stage and will be resolved as the painting progresses.

The texture and color of the ground are clear in the hair, which is painted with well-thinned blues and browns.

The ear remains unpainted, for an error in its positioning and size early on would involve lengthy correcting in the second session.

The color is more low-key or subdued than it will ultimately appear. High-key color can be applied in the second layer.

The bright white collar is the lightest note in a carefully planned scale of tones.

Materials

Ultramarine Blue

Winsor Green

Cadmium Yellow

Yellow Ochre

Burnt Sienna

Titanium White

Cadmium Orange

Permanent Rose

4 ◀ Once the first layer of paint has dried, begin building up color more thickly with small, chunky strokes in a variety of opaque orange, red, and green tints. Observe the fat-over-lean rule, whereby the oil content of the second layer of paint is greater than the first. This gives the new layer flexibility and avoids any cracking or flaking.

5 ▲ Use a small sable brush for the lines of the eye, adding a fleck of creamy yellow-white at the corner to indicate light shining on the eye socket. The black ground can be used for the eyebrow and iris of the eye, allowing detail to emerge without the need to define edges too sharply.

6 ▶ Now paint the ear, paying close attention to its measurements. At the center of the composition, the ear is an important feature in a profile portrait and accurate placement is essential if a likeness is to be successfully achieved. Its addition has the immediate effect of making the portrait more three-dimensional. Use a small round bristle brush, such as a No. 2, to paint the warm contours and dark shadows, before adding thick highlights with a small sable brush.

7 ▶ Use a small sable brush for texturing the hair. The soft brush is ideal for applying loose, relaxed stokes of color to suggest the fall of light across the thick curls. Apply purples and greens; these will appear pale against the transparent Ultramarine Blue, with much of the black ground still visible. This allows the distinctive thickness and body of the hair to emerge with the minimum of brushwork.

8 ◀ Using a medium-sized round bristle brush, such as a No. 6, strengthen the lights and darks of the neck with long brushstrokes to capture the smooth muscular form.

9 ▶ Add a second layer of cool, pale blue-gray to the background, including a little yellow for the subtle integration of the background and face. Blend the paint using a small round bristle brush, taking extra care where the background meets the outline of the face.

EARLY PROFILES

In Ancient Roman times, the art of painting was said to have originated when a woman drew the profile of the young man she loved by marking the lines of his shadow. Roman coins often bore profile images of heads of state and the tradition continues today.

HISTORY

Among the greatest profile images are the portrait of the Duke of Urbino in Piero della Francesca's Urbino Altarpiece in the Brera Art Gallery, Milan, Alesso Baldovinetti's *Portrait of a Lady in Yellow* in the National Gallery, London, and Filippo Lippi's *Portrait of a Man and a Woman at a Casement* in the Metropolitan Museum of Art, New York.

SILHOUETTES

The profile image is a marker of a kind of objective truth, and this may explain the tradition of having silhouette profiles made of all the members of a family through several generations.

10 ▲ Using a medium-sized round bristle brush, add a second, thicker layer of crisp blue-white to the collar with broad, sweeping brushstrokes. This accentuates its stiff texture and, where the light catches the front of the collar, makes a powerful tonal contrast with the dark brown vest. The smooth white also warms the dappled reds of the flesh tones.

11 ▷ Pick out final details, such as the highlight on the upper lip, using a small sable brush to apply color finely. Observe your sitter closely, noticing that the soft contours of the lips do not catch light as sharply as the clean, defined edges of the ear and nostril. Take time to get the final touches exactly right.

Profile on a black ground

The finished portrait gives a good solid impression but has not been over-refined. One might imagine the artist using this as a study for a larger painting of the sitter. Colors are generally cool in the highlights, with alternating strokes of warm and cool colors in the lights and shadows. The overall warmth of color is concentrated in the upper features, while the hair and cheek are predominantly cool. The painting retains a loose, chunky feel in the brushwork, which gives it movement and life.

Controlled brushwork has kept the highlights pure and unsullied by the surrounding colors.

The fall of light has been closely observed; it shines across the top half of the head, over the temple, eye, and nose, then down across the ear, neck, and collar.

Loosely applied highlights of opaque purple give the hair a distinctive texture and body.

A second layer of cool blue-gray helps keep the background flat and solid, while warming the flesh tones of the face and neck.

Nahem Shoa

Materials

No. 2 round bristle brush

No. 1 round sable brush

No. 3 round bristle brush

No. 6 round bristle brush

GALLERY OF COLOR

MUCH OF THE ATMOSPHERE of a portrait is generated by the way in which color has been used. It can make a painting shine with light and warmth, as in van Gogh's *L'Italienne*, where yellow, orange, and orange-red are complemented with touches of blue and green, or it can create a tender, gentle atmosphere, as it does in Leonard McComb's portrait of his mother. In Andrew Tift's *Birmingham Bus Driver*, color causes the work to vibrate with a strong intensity, while in Roger Oakes's self-portrait, color flows around the figure and creates a rich textural interweaving between figure and ground. In Polly Lister's painting, the red glows with a powerful sense of urban drama behind the artist in his black jacket.

Vincent van Gogh, *L'Italienne,* **1887** *32 x 23³/₄ in (81 x 60 cm)*
The extraordinary sense of directness that characterizes the portraits of van Gogh is present in this painting. Here, the woman's head is the focus of the work at the apex of a triangle that provides the solid structure for the figure. It is separated from the richly textured passage of color in the lower half of the figure by the paler tones of the blouse. The blue of the chair back sets off the warm orange-yellows, while the green in the whites of the woman's eyes seems perfectly natural.

Leonard McComb, RA, *Portrait of the Artist's Mother,*
Mrs. Delia McComb, **1993** *36 x 30 in (91.5 x 76.2 cm)*
There is a genuine sense of tenderness toward the subject in this work. The artist has built up the image with controlled touches of opaque color against the dark ground. He has used tints of purple and green, complementing them with warmer tints of orange-yellow and pinks, and the face emerges as a delicate and dignified image. The scarf, painted in deeper tints, gives body to the figure, spanning the two vertical sides of the canvas.

The eye has been beautifully observed and drawn in this detail. There is a far-away look and a watery physicality that shows the artist's concern with painting his sitter exactly as she is.

Polly Lister, *Vegetable Monitor*
30 x 30 in (76¹/₂ x 76¹/₂ cm)
The strong color effects of this work are created by the dramatic juxtaposition of red with black. The face has been painted almost monochromatically, using tints of purplish red and touches of the background red.

Andrew Tift, *Birmingham Bus Driver,*
54 x 37 cm (21¹/₄ x 14¹/₂ in)
This vigorous portrait brings together the driver and his bus in an extremely effective composition that links the various spaces of the interior of the bus with the world outside it. The painting relies for much of its effect on the contrast between orange-red and its complementary blue.

Roger Oakes, *Self-Portrait with Fatty-Grey and Sam* *30 x 12 in (76.3 x 30.5 cm)*
This rapidly painted study has a looseness and freshness in the brushwork and use of color that overrides some slightly less comfortable areas, such as the hand and the nose. The artist has managed to retain the purity of individual hues within the rich impasted mixtures.

The background colors have been added after the figure has been painted. These warm oranges and pinks, boldly applied, bring the painting to life.

ARTIST & SITTER

The quality and direction of light is an important aspect of a portrait.

SITTING FOR A PORTRAIT can be just as arduous and demanding as painting one. In fact, it makes a lot of sense to put yourself into the role of model at least once to get an idea of the concentration and effort it involves. Many sitters are self-conscious, and it is often better not to let them know which part of the portrait you are working on. Always give sitters regular rests, so that they can get up, wander around, and take refreshment. They may even like to look at the progress of the portrait, although some artists prefer not to show their work to the subject until it is finished. However, a kind of complicity can develop between artist and sitter if both are actively involved in the project, and this can be very positive as the painting progresses.

Positioning the sitter
In his "Notes on Painting" (1673-1699), William Gandy describes how the seventeenth-century painter Sir Peter Lely (Lilly) set up his studio for portrait work. The sitter would be positioned about 6 ft (1.8 m) into the studio from the principal source of light, a large, high window.

6 ft (1.8 m)

Recommended distances
At first, you may make the mistake of working too close to your sitter to have a clear view of the whole area you wish to feature in your portrait. About 6 ft (1.8 m) is an appropriate distance from your subject if you are painting a head and shoulders portrait, 10 ft (3 m) is sensible for a half-length portrait, while up to 18 ft (5.5 m) is traditional for a painting of a full-length figure.

10 ft (3 m)

Informal situations
Although it is helpful to bear in mind the recommended distances between painter and sitter, there are many informal situations when such guidelines are neither appropriate nor practical. You may, for instance, find yourself happily painting a couple of feet away from someone slumped in a chair, with bright afternoon sunlight casting deep shadows across their face. These images (*right*), show a relaxed and informal approach to portraiture, in which the artist responds to the unself-conscious, casual poses of the sitter.

18 ft (5.5 m)

The artist is positioned about 4 ft (1.2 m) from the sitter.

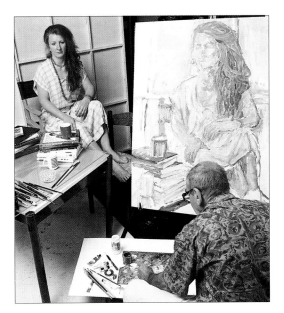

Large-scale work
When you are working on a large scale, it is useful to set up the canvas at an angle which allows you to see the model clearly and work on the whole image at the same time. Here, the artist is relatively close to the sitter for this informal full-length portrait (*see* pp. 44-47).

Eye levels
It is very important to establish the appropriate eye level of your sitter, for this will have a great effect on the tone of your portrait. Very often, the eye level of the artist and that of the sitter correspond. It is useful to make studies in which you experiment with eye levels to exaggerate the height of your sitter.

The artist looks down at the child.

The artist's eye level is far lower than that of the subject.

High and low viewpoints
Tall people seem even more statuesque if the artist paints them from a low viewpoint, while children look particularly small if painted from a high viewpoint.

The sitter is occupied by a source to the right, which creates an unself-conscious mood.

The artist moved farther away from the sitter and adopted a low viewpoint.

41

THE BODY

ANYONE WHO DOES a lot of life drawing and painting will know that the body is constantly surprising us. You may feel you have made studies of models of all ages, from all angles, and in all lights, and yet the experience of each new situation remains an entirely unique one. There is no short route to mastering the structure and proportion of the body; you can only build up your understanding by practicing continually. Make full-length sketches of people in the street, on the beach, moving and at rest, clothed and unclothed. Concentrate on the basic forms and how they relate to each other before you consider the details. Initially, you may find your heads are out of proportion, or that the arms seem too short, but the more you sketch, the more you will see how everything fits together.

Rapid sketches in pen and ink will help you understand the structure and proportion of the human body.

Make studies of figures sitting and reclining.

Understanding balance

Try to express a sense of the body's volume and weight by making studies of the same pose. Here, the weight is clearly concentrated on the left leg, and a real sense of solidity and balance has been achieved.

Detailed study

In this warm, vigorous study for a full-length oil portrait (*see* p. 56), there is an almost intimate bond between the figure, the chair, and the desk, with the composition well worked out. However, the artist has tried an alternative left arm and hand, and it is interesting to consider why he was unhappy with the original positioning. Perhaps it tightened up the portrait in an unintended way.

Painting hands

For every portrait you paint that includes a pair of hands, you will find a new position for them. Here, the subject is holding his hands out as if in the middle of expounding a theory. This creates an interesting challenge for the artist, not only because the hand is foreshortened (*below*), but also because the unusual pose needs to be painted well in order to look convincing. The palm is painted in shadow, which allows the fingers to be seen protruding. High-key greens and pinks have been used in the flesh tones to pull the hand forward from the figure.

Hands and feet

It is worth taking time to consider hands and feet separately from the rest of the body. Draw and paint detailed studies from life, using your own left hand if you are right-handed, and your own bare feet. You might also copy images from illustrations of the works of well-known artists.

If you are preparing for a three-quarter length or full-length portrait that features hands or feet, make fully modeled studies in oil color.

Make fully modeled color studies of hands held in various positions.

Seated figures

The seated figure is a common subject for portraiture. Make studies in which you try to capture the way the proportions of the figure alter as the body weight is adjusted.

Paint studies of feet, both in pairs and singly.

Foreshortening

If you are drawing someone who is sitting a short distance away and their arm or leg is extended toward you, this part of their body will appear proportionately much larger than the rest. This effect is known as foreshortening and is useful to bear in mind when you are working, for it is easy to fall into the habit of drawing what you think you should see rather than what you actually see.

43

EXPRESSIVE HIGH-KEY COLOR

THIS FULL-LENGTH study of a pensive red-haired woman is an example of alla prima painting on a white ground. The artist has incorporated a high-key palette of bright colors, with warm oranges and cool blue-green tints predominating. Their true colors are revealed against the white ground, and this is particularly effective where the paint has been used thinly. The warm colors are concentrated around the head and hair, forming the focus of the work. The artist constantly exploits complementaries, first laying down a fierce, vibrant color, then tempering it with its cool complementary. The style of painting is characterized by loose, expressive brushwork for both the thin, transparent colors and the thicker, more opaque ones.

Warm orange and red are complementaries of cool green.

1 ▶ Sketch out the face and figure with a wash of Prussian Green and Yellow Ochre using a small sable brush. Stand back from the canvas as often as necessary to assess the body proportions. The loose nature of this preliminary mark-making will allow you to keep your options open as the figure begins to emerge. Roughly draw in the shapes of the eyes, eyebrows, and nose.

2 ▶ Use a small round bristle brush to block in the hair with well-diluted Cadmium Orange. Indicate the planes of the face with broad strokes of thin pinks and greens, keeping the tonal range fairly close.

3 ▲ Use loose, sketched brushwork to fill in the flesh tones of the hands with a small round bristle brush. Overlay darker tones with opaque pale violets to suggest form.

4 ◀ Now pay attention to the foreground still life. Sketch out the lines of the desk, books, and mugs before rapidly blocking in color. Use the end of a paintbrush to delineate the curves of the mug's handle. Keep detail brief so the foreground objects do not compete with the central focus of the sitter's face and hair.

5 ◄ Such relaxed brushwork and improvisations with color may not always be successful. Correct any errors by scraping off the paint with a palette knife or by wiping the area carefully with a rag dipped in solvent. You can then rework the area with fresh paint.

6 ▲ Use a small sable brush, such as a No. 2, to paint lines of dark red and green for the edges of the books. Apply thick, broad strokes of opaque color for the green of the table, using a large filbert bristle brush. These lines of deep, rich color, in addition to the dark red of the mug, will help establish a pattern of dark tone in the lower half of the portrait.

7 ◄ Use blue-greens to cool the shadows of the fingers and to suggest the knuckles before coloring the lighter areas with warm oranges and pinks. Work up the hands to completion before turning to other sections of the portrait. For the fingernails, use a small sable brush to apply single strokes of pale opaque pink, avoiding any precise detail.

8 ▷ Switch to a small round bristle brush to apply thick oranges and yellows to the hair. Keep brushwork loose and fluffy to emulate the way the hair naturally waves and falls. Apply a well-thinned layer of pink to the background, working briskly so that the whole surface is covered as quickly as possible.

TIPS

● Well-diluted paint gives you a freedom and immediacy normally associated with watercolor. It removes the temptation to overwork during the early stages and allows you to cover the whole surface area of the canvas very rapidly.

● Applying thin paint to a white ground gives high-key color a particular clarity, for the ground shines through and shows the true purity of each color.

● When working alla prima, do not do too much wet-in-wet overpainting, otherwise there will be a tendency for your colors to become muddy.

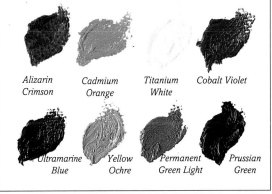

Alizarin Crimson

Cadmium Orange

Titanium White

Cobalt Violet

Ultramarine Blue

Yellow Ochre

Permanent Green Light

Prussian Green

9 ▲ Steadily build up color in the arms, avoiding meticulous blending but working wet-in-wet with a range of pink, blue, and yellow tints. Mix Titanium White and Cadmium Yellow for the highlights, stroking on the opaque color loosely using a small round bristle brush.

FORM

The way in which the painting has been made shows a somewhat unconventional approach to form. The image emerges from a series of sketchy, superimposed brushstrokes without any preliminary tonal modeling. There is no solid form as such, more a highly colored mosaic which, as you look at it, resolves itself into the figure of the young woman.

COLOR

The approach to color pays homage to Renoir and Bonnard, with orange, pink, lilac, and blue-green predominating. The high-key colors and loose, fluffy brushstrokes give the work a warm, relaxed feel.

MEANING

The model appears abstracted, as if lost in her own thoughts. The portrait, with its focus on the orange hair, reminds us of the way we look at other people through the focus of our own preoccupations or desires.

10 ◀ Paint the beads with thick dabs of Cadmium Orange using a medium-sized round bristle brush. The curve formed by the string of beads draws the eye back to the head, completing the central area of vivid color and strong tone. Work up the skin tones of the chest with chunky, dappled strokes of lilac, orange, and blue-green.

11 ◀ Use a medium-sized filbert bristle brush for the long, gentle strokes of the calves. Paint the shadows with blue-greens and use thick yellows and pinks for the areas that catch the light.

12 ▲ Add rich highlights of Cadmium Yellow and Cadmium Orange to the hair using a small filbert bristle brush. Scraped effects, achieved with the end of a paintbrush, add detail and texture to the hair.

13 ◀ Use a small sable brush to suggest form around the nostrils, eye sockets, and lips, without defining the lines too boldly. Work carefully, keeping brushwork light and deft.

14 ▶ Finally, apply a second layer of thin color to the background, tinting the pink with a little Cadmium Yellow. Apply broad strokes with a large filbert bristle brush.

Full-length figure with red hair

The finished portrait shows how an improvisational technique can allow expressive patterns of color effects to emerge gradually. The orange-reds of the hair are echoed in the background, which moves from warm pinks at the head to cooler purples and lilacs at the legs.

The mane of red hair is the most lively part of the portrait, the brushstrokes of rich color flickering in a blaze of orange-red.

The white ground glows through the thin paint of the dress and enhances the purity of the greens and yellows.

The cool lilacs of the lower background warm the skin tones of the legs while echoing the violets in the foreground details.

The sitter's left foot has been left unfinished, adding to the sense of spontaneity in the portrait.

Hans Schwarz

Materials

No. 2 round sable brush

No. 3 round bristle brush

No. 8 long filbert bristle brush

No. 6 long filbert bristle brush

No. 4 long filbert bristle brush

Palette knife

INTERPRETATION & MEANING

IN THE DESIRE to come to terms with the technical skills required for painting oil portraits, it can be easy to lose sight of other equally important considerations. When we work on a portrait, we should be aware that every choice made in relation to mood or atmosphere, composition and color, and background and setting, will have an impact on the meaning of the work. The meaning of a portrait, or the message it puts across, may well arise from the intuitions you get while actually painting. However, it is also the direct result of conscious decisions you have made in the setting up of the portrait. Try to work out exactly what you want to express in your work before you begin, and consider how a proposed change to the background or setting might affect how you interpret the painting, and how it is going to be perceived by others. It can be a useful exercise to take photographs of your sitter against different backgrounds and in various poses, as these will help you decide the best way to set up your portrait.

Creating a context
By seating the sitter at a café table, the image is immediately placed within a narrative context. If we then chose to paint the sitter looking down at her book with her coffee in front of her (*left*), we would be suggesting a relaxed and self-contained situation, in which all the action is concentrated within the sitter.

Choosing a pose
The context of an image changes dramatically according to the pose. If the sitter looks up (*far left*), the image takes on the quality of a film still, and we are invited to speculate on the possibilities that her expression generates. We can only wonder if it is one of wariness, annoyance, or distraction, for the subject of her attention remains a mystery.

Background colors
Often, a particular background is selected for the vivid color contrasts it sets up with the clothing and skin tones of the sitter. Here, the warm flesh tones stand out well against the cool, dark tones of the ivy, and the richly saturated red of the blouse perfectly complements the bottle-green foliage.

Eye contact
The direction of the sitter's gaze is an important clue to the message an artist wishes to get across. The sitter seems bemused (*right*), her face turned a little from the viewer and her eyes only half focused on some distant object. Alternatively, the head is held high and the spectator is fixed by a challenging, penetrating gaze (*far right*).

Portrait of Sergeant Bert Bowers

The subject of this painting by Leonard McComb, RA, was unknown to the artist before he began work on the portrait. Sergeant Bowers sat for him for a three-hour session every week over a period of five months. It is clear from the painting that during this long period the artist considered very deeply all aspects of the work, and in particular what it was that he wanted the portrait to say. There is a clarity and precision, which arises from the close attention that the artist has paid to every aspect of the portrait, including background and setting, and the pose and expression of the sitter. Each separate area of the canvas makes an important contribution to the overall image and is a necessary part of it.

Medals

The medals are a visual emblem of the campaigns fought by the old soldier. They seem not so much appended to the uniform as an integral part of it, woven into the fabric of the painting and of his life.

Pose and expression

The artist has chosen a direct, full-face pose for his sitter. There is no avoiding the cool, proud expression, which retains a certain energy although time has taken its toll. The fixed gaze seems partly concentrated on the present, and partly a mask for the thoughts and memories that must pass across the old man's mind.

Background

The patterning of the wallpaper gives a feeling of the background pushing forward toward the viewer. The texture seems to suggest a series of explosions, perhaps a reference to the sitter's wartime experiences. The orange-yellows in the core of the swirling, circular patterns and the flecks of orange-red underline this sense of the continual presence of the past.

Hands and stick

The impeccable white gloves, one worn and one held, give a poignancy to the flesh and bone of the hand as it emerges from the wide cuff. The hands rest decorously on the stick, which almost uncomfortably bisects the body. The hard, metallic texture of the stick calls to mind the barrel of a gun or the blade of a sword. It sets the tone of the pose and gives an edge to the meaning of the work.

COSTUME & DRAPERY

ARTISTS OFTEN TURN to the costume and drapery aspects of portraiture with a measure of relief after the rigors of painting flesh tones. Indeed, there is often a sense of relaxation in the drapery painting, with loose, easy brushwork and vibrant color effects. If you are setting up your portrait in a particular way, you may wish to decide what your sitter should wear. On the other hand, a portrait often reveals a greater accuracy of character and spirit if you allow the sitter to select his or her own clothing. However you proceed, the appearance and texture of costume and drapery will play an important part in the impact of the portrait.

Texture and pattern
The clothes your sitter wears and the accessories that go with them can be a rich source of texture, color, and pattern.

Postcard reference
Refer to illustrations from the history of portrait painting for wonderful examples of costume and drapery painting. These range from the ornate and highly intricate patterning featured in some early portraits to the intensity and vigor of costume by El Greco or van Gogh.

Establish the shape of the collar in white.

Sgraffito
This collar, after Rembrandt, shows a simple method of creating intricate detail. Lay down the dark background color and allow it to dry before you add the lighter color of the collar or scarf. While the paint is still wet, scratch the lacework design through it, using the sharpened end of a paintbrush handle or a knife.

Modeling wet-in-wet
This study, after El Greco, shows an unusual but effective method of painting drapery. After the initial sketching in Burnt Umber has dried, a thin uniform film of translucent crimson is applied. The subsequent modeling of tones is made while this layer is still wet, with transparent color used for the shadows and opaque white used for the light tones. The result is loose, rugged-looking drapery.

Scratch out the lines of the lace patterning.

The image is sketched in with Burnt Umber.

A thin transparent crimson is added.

Darker transparent tones are applied.

Opaque white is used for the modeling.

Glazing effects

This rich purple dress has been painted in two stages. The shape and form of the garment has been modeled monochromatically in pale blue and allowed to dry thoroughly. A translucent purple glaze has then been painted over it, giving a deep resonance to the color and a dimensionality to the costume.

The brushstrokes used to paint the form of the dress are loose and direct, with very little blending.

The deep, dark tones of the glaze color give depth to the modeling of the flower shapes around the shoulders and arms.

Rich patterning

If you are painting clothing with a rich patterning, begin by modeling the overall form and shape of the garment before you add the lines of the patterning. To retain the purity of the overlaid color, you can paint the patterning in white first, allow it to dry, and then add the required color. The final stage suggests the characteristic woven texture of the brocade fabric with delicate touches of Titanium White.

The patterning is painted in white.

A layer of red is added.

ACCESSORIES

The kinds of accessories people wear give clear clues to their character. Glasses, earrings, brooches, rings, cuff links, tie pins, and bracelets can be great revealers of personality. If your sitter wears glasses, consider how you want to paint them, for your approach will affect the tone of the portrait.

Glasses worn high on the bridge of the nose become an inseparable part of the face.

Glasses perched on the end of the nose form a barrier between sitter and viewer.

A contemplative mood is created when glasses are treated as a prop.

51

PAINTING IN LAYERS

THIS PORTRAIT WAS COMMISSIONED to honor the retirement of a distinguished headmaster. It is a formal work, showing the subject in his robes and in the school setting, but at the same time it is an attempt to focus on the humanity of the man himself. In preparation, the artist made a series of charcoal drawings and small oil studies of the head and shoulders. He also took a number of photographs for reference. For the portrait itself, an indirect, layered technique is used, with finely blended brushwork and light glazing. Close attention has been paid to the details of the background and costume. During the course of several sittings, the figure emerges with a strong, solid presence.

Preparatory drawing in charcoal

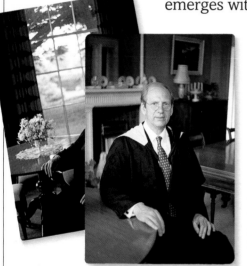

Reference material
For a commissioned portrait of this kind, it is very helpful to take photographs of your sitter from different angles and in a variety of lights and settings. There may also be areas of the painting, such as the background, which you will prefer to work up initially from photographs rather than from life.

1 ◀ Apply a Burnt Sienna imprimatura before sketching in the shape of the head with charcoal. Fill the area with Oxide of Chromium Green; this cool green ground will act as a counterpoint to the warm pink and brown flesh tones.

2 ▲ Build up the form of the face with Titanium White, using a medium-sized filbert bristle brush and a dry-brush technique. Stroke the ridges of the canvas with paint to create halftone effects. Gradually strengthen the depth and opacity of the white so that the shape of the face emerges more clearly; then leave to dry.

3 ◀ Mix flesh tones using touches of Cadmium Red and Cadmium Yellow Pale in Titanium White, adding Burnt Sienna for the deeper tones. Where the tones need to be cooler, use a little Winsor Blue or Green. At the same stage, give definition to the eyes with a small round sable brush, using Burnt Sienna for the outer ring of the iris and a touch of Cadmium Yellow Pale toward the pupil. This will give a useful early focus to the painting.

4 ▷ Use a similar technique for the hands as you used for the head, sketching in the modeling over the green ground with Titanium White. Fill the brush with the white paint, then wipe it off – this will leave enough residual paint in the hairs to allow you to use the dry-brush technique to advantage. Once the white has dried thoroughly, paint over it with flesh tones of a slightly thicker consistency.

5 ◁ Use a translucent mixture of Burnt Sienna with a touch of Winsor Blue and Permanent Rose to lay down the shadows of the suit and gown. Establish the lighter areas with opaque grays, using a medium-sized filbert bristle brush, such as a No. 6. Carefully work up tone and color before allowing the areas of costume to dry.

6 ▷ Now resume work on the head. Blend the flesh tones to the point where there is a general resolution of the main areas of light and shade. You may find that the tones need to be quite varied in order to achieve a lifelike, rounded modeling. Once this is completed, let the paint dry.

7 ◁ For the background areas, use translucent mixtures for the darker, shadowed areas and opaque mixtures for the light ones. A light mixture of Titanium White, Cadmium Yellow Pale, and Winsor Green is ideal for the bright foliage. Apply touches of color with a small filbert bristle brush, such as a No. 2.

8 ▲ Apply an overall glaze to the suit and robes, using Burnt Sienna, Winsor Blue, and Permanent Rose mixed with oil painting medium. Use a large filbert bristle brush, such as a No. 10, to brush on the color. The glaze will deepen the tone and give the blues and grays a rich glow.

COMMISSIONS

When you are working on commission, you need to establish at the outset what your fee will be and how you would like to be paid. Then you can get on with the job of painting the portrait.

SETTINGS

You may want your sitter to come to your studio, or you may prefer to paint your sitter in his or her own home environment. If you work at your subject's home, you will probably get a clearer and broader picture of them. You will also have the opportunity to paint them against a more personal and relevant background.

PAINTING STAGES

If you are painting in stages, your sittings should correspond to those stages and you will need to allow enough time between sessions for the paint to dry. If, on the other hand, you are working directly into the wet color, you will be able to paint your sitter on consecutive days. Set up at least one sitting for painting the final modifications and details.

9 ◀ Make any final adjustments to the clothes and drapery, such as the touch of light on the tie. Apply a mixture of Titanium White and Winsor Blue with a small round sable brush.

10 ◀ Make sure the paint on the head is completely dry before adding a very pale glaze to the area. Use a touch of transparent flesh color in oil painting medium for a subtle effect. Once the glaze has dried, you can pick out any final details, such as the sunlight on the right-hand side of the bottom lip.

11 ▲ Using a small round sable brush, such as a No. 1, paint a tiny highlight of Titanium White in the pupil. If any area of the canvas is still wet, rest your arm on a mahl stick as you work.

12 ▸ If your sitter wears glasses, it can be difficult to decide whether to paint him wearing them or not. One solution is to paint him holding a pair. Here, the reading glasses make an interesting detail at the bottom edge of the painting. Use a small round sable brush to pick out the bright, delicate lines of the wire frame.

Materials

Charcoal

No. 2 long filbert bristle brush

No. 1 round sable brush

No. 4 long filbert bristle brush

No. 6 long filbert bristle brush

No. 10 long filbert bristle brush

The foliage is built up in layers. The darker areas are painted before the lighter tones, and then the touches of high-key color are added.

Portrait of B.T. Bellis, The Leys School

In the finished portrait, the play of light is crucial to the way the work is perceived. Side light from a source on the right falls across the right side of the face as we look at it. This accentuates the features, giving a rugged look and strengthening the head as the central focus of the work. The head is also brought forward by the dark tones of the curtains immediately behind it.

A transparent purple glaze is applied to the suit and the robes, deepening the tone and enriching the colors.

Ray Smith

MAHL STICK

If you are unable to rest your arm or elbow on the edge of the canvas because the paint is wet, use a mahl stick. This is a stick of light bamboo or aluminum with a soft leather pad at one end, which rests on the canvas. A mahl stick allows you to keep your hand steady for painting while avoiding contact with the wet surface.

GALLERY OF FORMAL & INFORMAL POSES

A COMMISSIONED PORTRAIT does not have to be stiff and austere. On the contrary, many of the best portraits have an informality, even a tenderness, that shines through a relatively formal pose. Peter Greenham's painting of Mrs. Dorothy Hall and Whistler's portrait of his mother are good examples. On the other hand, the painting of Bruce Kent by Hans Schwarz has an informality of pose and setting that is not at all at odds with the strength of character of the sitter. Each of these paintings demonstrates the symbiotic relationship between artist and sitter, with the sitter's character emerging through the filter of the artist's style.

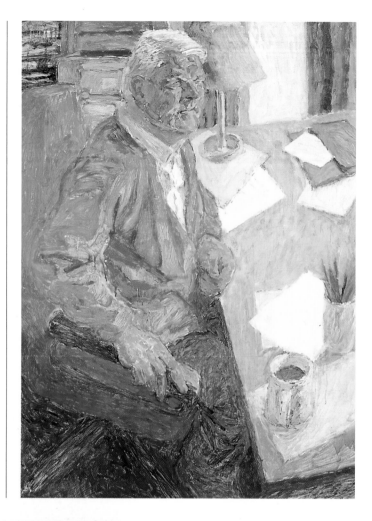

Hans Schwarz, *Bruce Kent*
48 x 36 in (122 x 91.5 cm)
The vision and humanity of the sitter shines through this energetic portrait. It shows a man who is comfortable and relaxed at his desk in his warm red cardigan and red chair, but who nonetheless demonstrates his strength of purpose in the expression in his eyes and in the way his large hand grips the arm of the chair. The mug of coffee planted firmly on the corner of the desk roots the work in the everyday.

James McNeill Whistler, *Arrangement in Grey and Black, the Artist's Mother*, 1871 *57 x 64¹/₂ in (145 x 164 cm)*
The dark, solid shapes of the wall, dress, and curtain give this portrait a formal poise and clarity. At the same time, there is a tenderness in the pose, with the head at a slight angle and the hands clasped together, and in the softness and warmth of the flesh tones set against the cool monochromatic tones of cap, dress, and wall. There is a reflective, almost elegiac tone about this painting that makes it a source of meditation.

Kees van Dongen, *La Comtessa de Noailles,* **1926** *77½ x 52 in (197 x 132 cm)*
There is an air of casual decadence about this portrait, which combines with the relaxed style of painting to create a work of great immediacy and charm. The use of pure black is unusual – most artists use mixtures of other colors to obtain dark tones – but it works perfectly in conjunction with the creamy white of the subject's bare shoulders and shimmering dress. The slim figure of the countess emerges dramatically from the deep shadows of the background, her face proud and amused.

Tonal and color contrasts are strong in this detail between the pale flesh tones and the deep red lips, choker, and cheeks.

Sir Peter Greenham, CBE, RA, *Mrs. Dorothy Hall,* **1960** *20 x 16 in (51 x 41 cm)*
Peter Greenham's paintings always seem to bring out the warmth and humanity of his subjects. He has a soft, flickering style, in which small brushstrokes dart around the contours and features of the sitter and eventually become resolved into his sympathetic portraits. Here, the mobility of style, coupled with a searching observation, gives great life to a subtle work.

In this detail, a kind and intelligent face emerges from the tentative, unblended brushstrokes.

COMPOSING A GROUP PORTRAIT

AS SOON AS YOU PUT TWO or more figures together in a portrait you enter a complex world of human interaction quite different from that of the single portrait. With double or group portraits, a series of relationships is being set up on the canvas, and the spectator will read these relationships in very specific ways. Whether you are using two or three figures to establish a particular narrative or coordinating a large family in a domestic portrait, you need to make clear decisions about composition.

The various stages of this group portrait demonstrate how comprehensive and careful your preparatory work should be.

Study in Conté crayon

Color sketches
In these preparatory studies, pencil, watercolor, and crayon have been used to explore elements of the composition. This is an excellent way to master the forms of the images to be used and to make practical color notes.

Pencil studies
Both small, swift pencil studies and detailed drawings of costume and accessories make useful reference material for painting the group portrait.

Detailed pencil and crayon drawing

Planning the composition
In this study, the artist begins to sketch out possibilities for the composition. At this early stage, there is a good sense of balance, but the background seems a little empty of figures. The hat worn by the woman on the left and the hair and clothing of the standing figure on the right have been established as the main areas of dark tone.

This self-possessed figure makes a youthful contrast to the older characters.

Watercolor study
A more highly resolved watercolor study shows how the composition has developed. The standing woman now leans over to talk to the woman in a hat, while a foreground figure has been added in the right-hand corner. The artist now considers the inclusion of several background figures, perhaps to fill out the composition.

Background figure
The addition of the old woman between two of the central figures will have the effect of leading the eye through the crowd toward the trees in the background.

Jane Allison

St. Pancras Garden Party
The final composition is a richly painted image full of life and activity. The bright, saturated colors and warmly observed figures give us a sense of being present at a real garden party. Here, there is neither overblown sentiment nor overcool detachment – more a feeling of showing a genuine human situation exactly as it is.

DRAMATIC LIGHT

Drawing your composition
After toning the canvas with a light wash of Raw Umber, rapidly sketch the outlines of the composition in a mix of Venetian Red and Raw Umber using a small sable brush.

THIS DOUBLE PORTRAIT is a central composition in which the eye is drawn into the frame, past the girls and to the open window. This is the source of the light that pours into the room, highlighting the girls' limbs and flooding the floor like a stage set. Indeed, there is a sense of the situation being consciously set up to celebrate these particular qualities of the light. The painting is completed in one session and does not need to be overworked to make its point. The artist has left out unnecessary detail, subdued the tones, and adjusted the colors to achieve a soft, warm effect.

1 ◀ Mix your colors from a palette of Raw Umber, Indian Yellow, Yellow Ochre, Cadmium Yellow Pale, Venetian Red, Ultramarine Blue, Titanium White, and Viridian Green. Use a medium-sized short flat bristle brush to cover each area of the canvas with deft strokes of broken color.

2 ▲ Establish early your areas of light and shade, and gradually build up tone and color, strengthening darker tones by working wet-in-wet with a long flat bristle brush. The shadows already contrast powerfully with the sunlit areas.

3 ▲ For the foliage in the garden outside, thin your colors with turpentine and apply delicate strokes of color with a small sable brush. Pale, dappled purple-grays and blues best express distant light and color.

4 ▶ Much of the theatrical atmosphere of this work is achieved by the strong sunlight dazzling the faces and limbs of the girls. Lighten your flesh tints with Titanium White and Cadmium Yellow Pale for opaque highlights on the faces, arms, and legs. Capture the gentle contours of the children's limbs by applying strokes carefully with a small sable brush.

TIPS

● Children can be restless sitters, so keep sessions as short as possible and use photographs and sketches for reference.

● If you prefer a layered technique, you can use well-thinned acrylics for the underpainting – they are fast-drying and will save you time.

5 ▶ The bold definition of the window frame holds our attention in the central area of the composition. The effect is softened by the gentle curves and light texture of the curtains. Apply thick dashes of yellow and white to the edges directly lit by the sun. A small sable brush allows the control and precision necessary for the finer highlights.

Materials

No. 2 round sable brush

No. 2 short flat bristle brush

No. 3 long flat bristle brush

No. 5 short flat bristle brush

6 ▲ Use a short flat bristle brush, such as a No. 2, to paint the deep shadows of the floor with long, flat strokes of dark browns and muted purple-grays. These areas of deep shade act as smooth, solid anchors in the lower half of the composition and contrast dramatically with the streaks of sunlight below.

7 ◀ Blend the broken colors of the wallpaper for a sleek, flat appearance, before picking out final highlights with a small sable brush. Keep details, such as the patterning on the wallpaper, to a minimum.

Double portrait with dramatic light
The finished painting shows the successful effect of combining muted yellows with complementary lilacs and purple-grays. The bright light seems to hold the two girls in its warmth and clarity, expressing a quality of timelessness in childhood. The work speaks of a single, casual moment when, for an instant at least, time is suspended.

The soft brushwork on the arms expresses the gentle contours of the children's limbs.

The strong squares of the box and window form a central focal point in the painting.

Deep shadows contrast with the areas of sunlight.

James Horton

FURTHER STUDIES

Use your finished work as a study for more detailed paintings. This version, painted on a larger canvas with finely blended brushwork, is much sharper in detail. The girl's raised arm adds a sense of immediate action and energy.

GALLERY OF DOUBLE PORTRAITS

THE DOUBLE PORTRAIT invariably invites speculation or suggests observations about the nature of human relationships. Settings become enormously important, containing clues to guide our thoughts and reactions. The themes and relationships at work in these four portraits are quite varied. We see the self-possession of children at play, the intimacy of the relationship between mother and child, a portrait of the artist's parents, which is at once clear and enigmatic, and two men in an unidentified space lit by artificial light. All four portraits share that quality of attraction which invites our curiosity.

John Singer Sargent, *Carnation, Lily, Lily, Rose,* 1885-6 *68¹/₂ x 60¹/₂ in (174 x 153.7 cm)*
The artist has painted the girls during those twilight moments when the atmosphere is at its most dreamlike with the combination of natural and artificial light. Each girl is absorbed in the lantern she holds, yet there is a camaraderie in this shared activity that gives the painting warmth.

Neale Worley, *Harold and Dennis* *30 x 36 in (76.2 x 91.5 cm)*
The undefined relationship between the two figures makes this work particularly interesting. What we see clearly is how their physical proximity brings out the character of each man. The foreground figure faces the artist and the spectator, and there is a degree of humanity expressed which invites a dialogue with us. The second man looks down, his face a deeper tone, as if closer to the shadows.

There is an ease and an assurance in the artist's brushwork, which gives the hand a great deal of life and vigor. We can imagine it moving up to express a point or to bring the cigarette up to the face.

Ghislaine Howard, *Mother Embracing Her Child* *47 x 37 in (119.5 x 94 cm)*
The subject of mother and child has been a central one in the development of oil painting. Here, we see the theme approached from a completely informal point of view. There is an immediacy and a joy about this work that truly expresses the mother's love for the feel and the smell of her baby. The warmth and informality of the relationship is shown as much by the style of the work, with its rich charcoal drawing and loosely sketched brushwork, as it is by the subject itself.

The intimacy of the bond between mother and child is expressed in the angle of the mother's head, leading us to wonder what she is whispering to her child.

David Hockney, RA, *My Parents,* 1977 *72 x 72 in (182.9 x 182.9 cm)*
David Hockney's portrait of his parents has the characteristic crispness of all his painting. He has set them up with the clarity of a still life by Chardin, a book of whose work lies on the shelf, or an image by Piero, whose painting we see in the mirror. We wonder about the nature of their relationship and their relationship with their son. His mother gazes directly at the painter, but his father has moved his chair to a position that suits him, and he is entirely absorbed in his book. Two very distinctive characters emerge.

The artist's mother is alert and kind in this detail; she faces the artist directly, giving him her full attention.

63

ALTERNATIVE TECHNIQUES

EVERY ARTIST MAKES a unique contribution to the medium in which he or she works, and it is a tribute to the extraordinary variety of oil paint effects and techniques that we can immediately recognize the individual styles of so many different painters. You will find that as you continue to paint portraits, you quite naturally develop your own technical and stylistic approach. This will lead to your using oil color in ways that no one else has. Here, two alternative techniques for making oil portraits are demonstrated. The first involves a simple sgraffito method on sand-blasted glass, and the second shows how a freeze-frame image from a video can inspire an unusual portrait.

Texturing oil paints
You can experiment with different textures by stirring sand or sawdust into your paints. Be sure to use a rigid support.

Portrait study
This small sketchbook image was made in a few seconds with a fine-nibbed pen. Its simple lines are recreated in a portrait on sand-blasted glass (*below*).

1 ▲ Wash and dry a piece of sand-blasted glass and coat the sand-blasted side with Titanium White oil color straight from the tube. Use a thin, flexible piece of plastic, such as an old credit card, to spread the paint evenly and thinly over the back of the glass. Use the sharpened end of a brush handle to draw the image into the paint with a steady hand. Make sure you are scraping along the surface of the glass as you draw.

2 ▶ Allow the paint to dry completely; this may take a few days. Apply thick dark color to the lines you have scraped out, using a large bristle brush.

3 ◀ When the dark color has dried, turn the glass over, and you will see the lines of the portrait image against the completely uniform white ground. The sand-blasted glass gives a soft, slightly grainy effect to the lines. The particular quality of the image depends to a large extent on the thickness of the glass, which can give an attractive greenish or bluish cast to the work. "Back-painting" on glass is a traditional technique, and you can make fully three-dimensional-looking images if you wish. Always remember that you are painting in reverse, so you need to start with the highlights and light opaque tones and work back to the shadows.

OIL STICKS

Oil sticks, made from oil paints blended with waxes, are an excellent medium for painting full-color portraits. You can use them like crayons, but you will find they have a far greater intensity of color and a more liquid feel. It is possible to paint into wet color with an oil stick and retain the purity of the color you have added.

Freeze-frame portrait
Electronic imagery can provide a stimulating source of inspiration for the contemporary portrait painter. In this monochromatic study, a textured gesso ground has been prepared on panel. This has then been sized and given a Winsor Green imprimatura. The image is painted in Titanium White using brushstrokes that imitate the flickering images of a video freeze-frame. You can experiment with the color controls on your television set to produce source images in highly saturated colors.

The picture frame is an integral part of the portrait; it echoes the dark, solid edge of a television screen.

65

GALLERY OF MODERN APPROACHES

THERE HAS BEEN a great diversity of approach to portraiture during this century. Advances in electronic imaging and other forms of instant visual communication have created exciting new possibilities for many painters. Howard Hodgkin is among those who best express their insights into character by using a nonfigurative style, while artists such as Frank Auerbach continue to work directly from life, but in quite innovative ways.

Frank Auerbach, *JYM1.1981,* 1981 *22 x 20 in (56 x 50.8 cm)*
A unique approach to portraiture and a process of continual readjustment lie behind this work by Frank Auerbach. The artist uses the same few models repeatedly for his paintings; he knows them well and considers it important to see them in contexts other than the studio. By this means, he is able to build up a picture of his subjects that informs the painting sessions in the studio. Here, thick, loosely mixed oil color is applied vigorously and swiftly to produce a portrait of astonishing immediacy.

Patricia Wright,
Blue Self-Portrait *9 x 6¹/₄ in (23 x 16 cm)*
In this self-portrait, Patricia Wright looks back at the viewer with a rather guarded expression. There is an air of wariness, as if she is uncertain about the outcome of this confrontation. She gives us few clues; her clothes are black and rudimentary in form, and her hair is pulled back under a cap. The background has been textured, overpainted, and then scraped back, so that it becomes a powerful, almost aggressive feature of the painting.

A tension is set up between the sensitivity of the flesh tones and the coarse, textured background.

Max Beckmann, *Portrait of an Argentinian,*
1929 *49¹/₄ x 32³/₄ in (125 x 83.5 cm)*
In Max Beckmann's paintings, the realities of life
are transformed into the stuff of legend, myth, and
metaphor. His characters inhabit a strange metaphysical
world in which our unconscious preoccupations are
given dramatic expression. Something of this is revealed
in the pale, sensitive young man dressed in his dinner
jacket and poised on a chair. Beckmann has captured
a sense of uneasy nonchalance and a restlessness of
spirit that gives his sitter an enigmatic character.

In this detail, the man's face is almost
white, his cheeks flushed pink, and his
lips orange-red, suggesting a night
person always seen in artificial light.

Howard Hodgkin, *Mr. and Mrs. Stephen Buckley,*
1974-6 *28³/₄ x 42¹/₄ in (73.3 x 107.3 cm)*
We can only guess from the free-floating forms and bright colors
of this abstract painting exactly what the artist wishes to say about
his subjects. A certain boldness and a ruggedness of construction
point the way to our interpretation of the double portrait.

The circular crimson
brushstrokes of this
detail have a vigorous,
scratched look,
creating a rugged
form that acts as
a gateway to the
dark space behind.

VARNISHING & FRAMING

VARNISHING A PAINTING gives it some protection from dust, dirt, and abrasion. The main difference between a layer of varnish and the layers of paint is that paint layers are permanent, whereas the varnish is removable. In future years, when the varnish gets dirty, discolors, or degrades, it can be removed and new varnish can be applied. Oil painting varnishes generally consist of ketone resins in solvent, and these are available as gloss or matte varnishes. Alternatively, you can use wax varnishes made from beeswax and solvent, which provide good protection and give a lustrous appearance. Choose your frame with great care. A sympathetic frame will enhance a portrait, while an inappropriate choice can rob the image of its impact.

Your choice of frame will have a considerable effect on the look and mood of a portrait.

VARNISHING

Use a flat brush to apply two coats of varnish. The brushstrokes used for the second coat should be at right angles to those of the first. If you use a wax varnish, polish the surface gently when dry.

Allow the varnish to dry before applying the second coat.

Varnish

Frame moldings
There are countless picture frame moldings available commercially. You can also ask a good picture frame maker to create a unique frame for your portrait.

1

2

3

4

Choosing a frame
The best way to decide which style of molding to choose for your frame is to experiment with prefabricated corners. Of those tried here, the heavy wooden frame (1) works best, its muted yellow emphasizing the blue in the background color and enriching the flesh tones. The simple lines of the top left molding (5) are also successful, but the red version (8) is less appropriate, its color too strong for the subtle colors of the painting. Also unsympathetic are the two slim, dark moldings (6, 7), for their scale has little effect on so striking an image. The chosen frame is bold and solid; it powerfully maximizes the impact of a highly dramatic pose.

The simple wooden corner (1) works better than the more detailed styles.

Creating a focus

The thick wooden frame is designed to focus on the intensity of the color in this small painting, with the rich, natural texture of the wood enhancing the red ground. The square solidity gives the impression of the subject looking out of a window frame, which creates an intriguing mood of detachment.

Cardboard mats

Many of the pencil and charcoal studies you have made on paper will deserve to be framed behind glass. A cardboard mat provides a visual bridge between the work and the molding.

Sympathetic framing

The simple clarity of this portrait is well retained by the use of a flat wooden molding. The gray stain echoes the earth colors used in the painting itself.

5   7

6   8

The dark corners look too thin for the chunky image and the red too overpowering.

The ridged texture of the chosen frame echoes the dappled brushwork.

GLOSSARY

ACETATE Clear plastic film on which it is possible to draw in ink.

ADJACENT COLORS Colors with some similarity in hue. A warm orange-red and a warm orange-brown might be juxtaposed in a painting to give a quite different kind of color harmony than that achieved by using complementaries. The term also refers to any color next to another one.

ALLA PRIMA Literally means "at first" and is a direct form of painting made in one session or while the color remains wet. (As opposed to "indirect" painting in which the painting is built up in layers.)

BRISTLE BRUSHES Made from hog hair, these are brushes with stiff, coarse hairs that hold plenty of thick paint and retain their shape well.

BROKEN COLOR Color that has been changed by mixing with another color or affected optically by the juxtaposition or superimposition of another color.

CHARCOAL Carbonized wood made by charring willow, vine, or other twigs in airtight containers. If charcoal is used for a preparatory drawing, the excess dust can be rubbed off the surface using a large sable brush or a piece of doughy bread.

COLOR HARMONY The balance and order of color in a painting, created by the artist's manipulation of such effects as warm and cool colors, complementary colors and high-key and low-key colors.

COMPLEMENTARY COLORS Opposite colors on the color wheel of maximum contrast to each other, such as yellow and blue-violet, orange-red and blue, or magenta and green. In painting, if you were physically to mix two complementary colors together, you would get black.

DARKS Those parts of a painting that are in shadow.

DRY-BRUSH TECHNIQUE A method of painting in which paint of a dry or stiff consistency is stroked or rubbed across the canvas. It is picked up on the ridges of the canvas or the texture of the painted surface, leaving some of the color below still visible.

EGG TEMPERA Painting medium consisting of pigment and distilled water bound with egg yolk.

EPIDIASCOPE Projector for enlarging sketches or reproductions.

FAT-OVER-LEAN A fundamental rule for producing a sound paint structure. It applies to oil painting in layers, in which each subsequent layer of paint has its oil content increased a little by the addition of oil painting medium, so that each layer is a little more flexible than the one beneath it.

FILBERT Bristle brush with a round toe and flattened metal ferrule.

FLAT BRUSHES Square-toed brushes with flattened metal ferrules.

FLAT COLOR An area of color of uniform, untextured tone.

FORESHORTENING The perspective effect that occurs when part of the subject is much closer to the artist than another part and appears large in comparison.

GESSO A traditional ground for oil painting on panel comprising animal glue (rabbit skin glue) and plaster of paris, chalk, or whiting. Prepare the size in a double boiler using 2½ oz (70 grams) of size to 2 pts (1 litre) of water, apply this to the panel and allow to dry. Stir in plaster of paris to a creamy consistency and apply several coats to the panel. Sand to a smooth finish and add a second coat of size to reduce the absorbency of the panel.

GLAZE A film of transparent or translucent oil color laid over another dried color or underpainting.

GROUND The surface on which color is applied. This is usually the priming rather than the support.

HALFTONES Transitional tones between the highlights and the darks.

HIGH-KEY COLOR Brilliant and saturated color. Some oil colors, especially the transparent ones, are dark when used directly from the tube, so a little white can be mixed with them to give a saturated color effect. Alternatively, such colors can be used thinly on a white ground for a similar high-key look.

HIGHLIGHT The lightest tone in drawing or painting. In oil painting techniques, white constitutes the lightest tone.

HUE This describes the actual color of an object or substance in terms of its position on the color wheel. The hue may be red, yellow, blue, green, and so on.

IMPASTO A thick layer of paint, which is heaped up in ridges to create a heavily textured surface.

IMPRIMATURA A thin overall film or stain of translucent color over a white priming. This is applied before the artist begins to paint. It does not affect the reflective qualities of the ground, but it provides a useful background color and makes it easier to paint between the lights and darks.

Alla prima

Oil colors

Grounds

LOW-KEY COLOR Subdued, unsaturated color that tends toward brown and gray. Tertiary colors are low-key in appearance and produce neutral hues similar in mood and tone.

MODELING In painting techniques, indicating the three-dimensional shape of an object by the appropriate distribution of different tones.

MONOCHROMATIC PAINTING Painting in tones of one color.

OPAQUE PAINTING The opposite of transparent painting, whereby lighter tones are produced by using white paint and not by thinning the paint.

PALETTE (i) Portable surface for mixing colors. Mahogany palettes are useful for portrait painting if you are working on a warm brown ground, because the mixed colors appear on the palette as they will on the canvas. (ii) The range of colors an artist chooses to work with.

PIGMENT Solid, colored material in the form of small discrete particles.

PRIMER The preliminary coating laid onto the support prior to painting. A layer of primer protects the support from any potentially damaging components of paint and provides the surface with the right key, absorbency, and color before painting.

PROPORTION The correct or appropriate relationship between the parts and the whole.

ROUND BRUSHES Brushes with rounded toes and round metal ferrules.

Preparatory drawing

SABLE BRUSHES Soft, fine brushes made from tail hair of sable. These are used for detailed brushwork or final touches and highlights.

SAND-BLASTED GLASS Glass sprayed with abrasives under pressure to make the surface translucent and finely textured.

SATURATION The degree of intensity of a color. Colors can be saturated, i.e. vivid and of intense hue, or unsaturated, i.e. dull and tending towards gray.

SGRAFFITO A drawing or pattern-making technique of scratching through a layer of wet paint with a tool such as the sharpened end of a paintbrush handle to reveal another, dry color below it.

SIZE Rabbit skin or other glue used to protect canvas from the potentially damaging effects of oil in the paint before priming and to seal or reduce the absorbency of wooden panels. The binding material for gesso.

SOLVENT Any liquid in which a solid can be dispersed to form a solution. A resin varnish dissolved in an organic solvent like turpentine will harden after being applied as the solvent evaporates. Used widely as thinners or diluents.

SUPPORT The material on which a painting is made. Almost any surface can be used, but artists tend to use either a wooden panel or a canvas. These materials are available in a range of textures and weights.

TINT Color mixed with white.

TONE The degree of darkness or lightness of a color.

TONED GROUND An opaque layer of colored paint of uniform tone applied over the primer before starting the painting.

UNDERPAINTING Preliminary painting, over which other colors are applied.

Imprimatura

VARNISH Protective surface over a finished painting imparting a glossy or matte surface appearance.

WARM AND COOL COLORS Generally, a color such as orange-red is considered warm. In accordance with atmospheric or aerial perspective, warm colors appear to advance toward the viewer.

WET-IN-WET Working with wet paint into wet paint on the surface of the support.

Opaque color mixes

A NOTE ON COLORS, PIGMENTS, AND TOXICITY

In recommending Winsor Blue and Winsor Green (which are trade names of the Winsor & Newton Company) we are recommending "Phthalocyanine" pigments; other artists' material manufacturers refer to them by their own trade names. These include Phthalo Blue and Green, Monestial Blue and Green, and so on. Similarly, in recommending Permanent Rose we are recommending a "Quinacridone" pigment. If you have any doubts about which pigment you are buying, refer to the manufacturer's literature.

We have tried to avoid recommending pigments, such as the Chrome colors, which carry a significant health risk. Toxic pigments such as Lead White or Cobalt Blue should also be avoided when making your own colors. In the case of colors such as the Cadmiums, however, there is nothing commercially available which matches them for color and permanence. But there is no danger in their use nor in that of other pigments provided artists take sensible precautions.

Solvents are damaging to your health, so always keep the lids of solvent jars screwed on tight and use only as much as you need. The long-term effects from inhaling the fumes of distilled turpentine include loss of memory, the inability to follow an argument, and paranoia.

A NOTE ON BRUSHES

The brush sizes given here refer to Winsor & Newton brushes. They may vary slightly from those of other manufacturers.

INDEX

ACKNOWLEDGMENTS

Author's acknowledgments
Ray Smith would like to thank everyone at Dorling Kindersley involved with the DK Art School series, especially my editor, Louise Candlish, and designer, Claire Pegrum, whose real interest in the project made them such an enthusiastic and efficient team. They were ably assisted by Margaret Chang and Dawn Terrey, with help from Ruth Kendall. Thanks to Alun Foster at Winsor and Newton Ltd for all his expert advice. In addition, I would like to thank all the artists who contributed to the book, including the Royal Academicians who kindly agreed to their work being represented in the book and the young painters whose work was featured in the National Portrait Gallery BP Awards exhibition and who created some exciting new work for this book. Thanks also to Lord and Lady Renfrew and to B.T. Bellis and the Leys School in Cambridge for lending paintings, and to John Butler for introducing me to Kees van Dongen's "Countess." Finally I would like to thank my daughter Emily for letting me use some of her very early drawings.

Picture Credits